OUR QUEST FOR IDENTITY

KINGDOM 101 FOUNDATIONS SERIES:
BOOK ONE

LONZINE L. LEE

OUR QUEST FOR IDENTITY

Our Quest For Identity - Kingdom 101 Foundations Series
Copyright © 2025 by Lonzine L. Lee
Print ISBN: 979-8-9872129-3-6
eBook ISBN: 979-8-9891027-4-7

Published by Dominion Unlimited Publications.
P.O. Box 1412, Manteca, California 95336
www.dominionunlimited.org
All rights reserved.

Cover design by David Munoz Prophetic Art. www.davidmunozart.com
Author photo by Mike Rodriguez kingdomphotography@yahoo.com.

All rights reserved solely by the author. The author guarantees all contents of this book are original and do not infringe upon any laws or legal rights of any other person or work, and that this book is not libelous, plagiarized or in any other way illegal.
No portion of this publication may be reproduced, stored in a retrieval system, or transmitted in any form by any means – electronic, mechanical, photocopying, recording or any other – except for brief quotations in printed reviews, without the express written consent or the permission of the author. Short extracts may be used for review purposes.
Unless otherwise noted, all scriptures are taken from the NKJV are taken from the NEW KING JAMES VERSION (NKJV): Scripture taken from the NEW KING JAMES VERSION®. Copyright© 1982 by Thomas Nelson, Inc. Used by permission. All rights reserved.
Scriptures marked AMPC are taken from the Amplified® Bible Classic, Copyright© 1954, 1958, 1962, 1964, 1965, 1987 by The Lockman Foundation. Used by permission. www.Lockman.org.
Scriptures marked KJV are taken from the King James Version (KJV): King James Version, public domain.
Scriptures marked CEV are taken from the CONTEMPORARY ENGLISH VERSION (CEV): Scripture taken from the CONTEMPORARY ENGLISH VERSION copyright© 1995 by the American Bible Society. Used by permission.

Scriptures marked ISV are taken from the INTERNATIONAL STANDARD VERSION (ISV): Scripture taken from INTERNATIONAL STANDARD VERSION, copyright© 1996-2008 by the ISV Foundation. All rights reserved internationally.

Scripture quotation marked *Mirror* is from *The Mirror Study Bible* © Francois du Toit, Kindle Edition (Mirror Word Publishing, 2018). Used by permission. All rights reserved. For more information, visit www.mirrorword.net

Scriptures marked NAS are taken from the NEW AMERICAN STANDARD (NAS): Scripture taken from the NEW AMERICAN STANDARD BIBLE®, copyright© 1960, 1962, 1963, 1968, 1971, 1972, 1973, 1975, 1977, 1995 by The Lockman Foundation. Used by permission.

Scriptures marked NEB are taken from THE NEW ENGLISH BIBLE. Scripture quotations taken from the New English Bible, Copyright © Cambridge University Press and Oxford University Press 1961, 1970. All rights reserved. Used by permission.

Scripture quotations marked NRSV are taken from the New Revised Standard Version Bible, copyright © 1989 National Council of the Churches of Christ in the United States of America. Used by permission. All rights reserved worldwide.

Scriptures marked TLV are taken from the Messianic Jewish Family Bible, Tree of Life Version. Copyright (c) 2015 by the Messianic Jewish Family Bible Society. Used by permission of the Messianic Jewish Family Bible Society." "TLV" and "Tree of Life Version" and "Tree of Life Holy Scriptures" are trademarks registered in the United States Patent and Trademark office by the Messianic Jewish Family Bible Society.

Hebrew word definitions come from the Ancient Hebrew Lexicon of the Bible.

Greek Dictionaries published in 1890; public domain.

Webster 1828 Dictionary definitions are sourced from Webster's Dictionary of American English (1828) – Online Edition, http://webstersdictionary1828.com.

Oxford English Dictionary definitions are taken from The Online Oxford English Dictionary. www.oed.com

Unless otherwise noted in footnotes, Greek definitions come from Thayer, J.

H. (2007). *Thayer's Greek-English Lexicon of the New Testament: Code with Strong's Concordance Numbers*. Hendrickson Publishers, Inc.

All headings, story artwork, and graphics listed below were generated from the imagination of Lonzine Lee, using AI technology via DALL·E by OpenAI, customized based on user-provided specifications. Copyright © May 30, 2025. Licensed to Lonzine Lee. All rights reserved.

- DNA Possibilities: Radiant DNA chapter heading background.
- Golden DNA Strands Parts heading background
- DNA In Miniature scholar heading background
- ESDSS graphic.
- *REENA'S QUEST* Cover

CONTENTS

Acknowledgments	ix
Forewords	xv
About The Kingdom 101 Foundations Series	xxiii
Oral Traditions, Sayings, and Writings	xxvii

PART ONE

1. The Purpose Of Identity	3
2. Why A Quest?	11
3. The Weapons of Their Warfare	15
4. We Must Needs Ask	27
5. The Core Aspects Of Our Identity	35
6. The King Takes Center Stage	43
7. The Heart Of The King	51
8. The Image & Likeness Influence	57
9. The Imago Dei: From Moses to Jesus To You	69
10. Deposing The Counterfeit Identity	79
A Few Theological/Scholarly Comments On Mark 5	89
11. A Son Power Flex	95
12. The Story of You	111

Part II	123
13. My Jesus Encounter	125
14. Spiritual Disrupters	129
15. The Truth About Brokenness	143
16. Can You Handle The Truth?	151
17. Broken Pieces & Established Patterns	157
18. Repentance: The Superpower of Sons	169
19. A Second Repentance Spiritual Encounter	181

20. Sonship Must Be Manifested — 185
21. Familiar Patterns, Familiar Spirits — 199
22. The Power of The Wilderness — 207
23. The Frequency of A God-Controlled Spirit — 223
24. Our Sonship Identity — 229

Part III — 241

Appendix A — 242
Appendix B — 248
Appendix C — 251

REENA'S QUEST

Reena's Quest: The Mists of Duperie — 256
Endnotes — 267
About the Author — 273
Books by Lonzine L. Lee — 275

Thank You! — 276

ACKNOWLEDGMENTS

To my mother, Apostle Dr. Bacer J. Baker, thank you for introducing me to Jesus, and to the gospel of the Kingdom of God. Your insights and revelation regarding the spirit mind and the brain are epic and so vital to the manifestation of God's sons in the earth. Thank you for pouring into me the way that you do. I love you, Mommy. By the way, if any of what I say seems familiar to you, it is probably because you've preached it, so please, keep those messages coming. :)

Arayna Joyelle (aka Princess Reena), you are such a beautiful, talented, witty, wise, fabulous woman. I'm so proud to be your Mom. I love you, Baby Girl.

Bold statements call for acts of faith. Thanks to my *Divinely Designed* friends: Anita, Christal, Geneva, Lesley, LeTasha, Michele, and Xochitl, for the times we spent growing together. I praise God for each one of you amazing *21st Century Women*. I love you all.

Paul A. Moore, thank you, my beloved friend for flexing your superpowers with the tutorials and scholarly references found in your truly excellent book, *Thy Kingdom Come*, and for the historical Kingdom insights that you so freely share. *Let the Good Times Roll.*

Apostle Papa Eddie Maestas and Apostle Uncle Calvin Cook, I thank each of you for the outpouring of love, instruction, and correction that you have each given to me. I honor and love you both.

Thanks still go to the original folks that encouraged my first steps into self-publishing. Most of them have moved off planet, but the love is still felt.

And much love to my *MTEM/Astounding Love! A Global Church Fellowship & Training Center* family. You all inspire me to really live this Kingdom thing of ours. I love you all.

Truly, I am a blessed woman.

ENDORSEMENTS

Our Quest For Identity is a powerful and prophetic journey that ministers truth with raw clarity and profound spiritual insight. From the very first chapter, Lonzine L. Lee courageously opens a path to rediscovery and transformation by boldly declaring our origin, identity, and destiny as sons of God. This work is not merely informational—it is impartational. It challenges the reader to confront counterfeit mindsets, embrace spiritual sonship, and manifest Heaven's intent on Earth.

I was deeply moved by the authenticity and Spirit-led instruction throughout the manuscript. The author's fusion of biblical narrative, revelatory storytelling, and transparent testimony makes this book both unique and impactful. Particularly refreshing is the call to return to the King's language, to speak Heaven's vocabulary, and to live as Kingdom citizens with full authority and responsibility.

Yes, I absolutely intend to purchase and share this book when it releases—and I will also recommend it as a transformative course of study for leadership teams, discipleship groups, and those pursuing maturity in their walk with God. With the forthcoming workbook, this could serve as a foundational discipleship tool for equipping believers in the present-day move of God.

Lonzine L. Lee's writing awakens dormant truth and invites

readers to engage in their divine quest for manifested sonship. If you've ever felt misplaced in the crowd of religious labels or disillusioned by a powerless Christianity, *Our Quest For Identity* will recalibrate your focus to the eternal narrative of the King and His Kingdom. This is more than a book—it's a spiritual mirror and a divine summons.

—Dr. Barry Cook
Houston, TX, USA
The Leaders Edge Inc.
Author of *Mission-Minded Leaders*
Leadership Trainer | Kingdom Equipper | Apostolic Voice

This book is about answering the cry of creation. Even before you took your first breath, your image was established within your identity. This book is about image, identity, and who God says you are. Knowing how to truly become who God says you are includes learning not to let anything—addiction, misplaced desire, emotional struggle—detour you from manifesting that identity on Earth.

The journey laid out here in this book, *Our Quest For Identity* is mental, emotional, and spiritual. It's a roadmap to help you navigate the sewer of the soul and mind, and come into the cleansing rank of the spirit. In this first part of the five-book Kingdom foundational series, you are invited to begin your journey learning to operate out of spirit (unconscious), soul (subconscious), and body (conscious) to bring you into the spirit conscious son of God that you that you are.

The Earth is groaning for the manifestation of the sons of God. That means you. But not everyone will accept the King's challenge. Some will ignore it. Others will say yes and step into the fight of faith to fully manifest their true identity. The question this book asks is simple: Which part of you rules—flesh or spirit? Which identity are you most comfortable living? This book dares you to answer that.

—Apostle Bacer J. Baker
More Than Enough Ministries, Inc.
Host, *Tell It Like It Is: The Kingdom of God Way*
Manteca, CA USA

I find Lonzine L. Lee's book, *Our Quest for Identity*, to be a powerful tool to help readers guide their thoughts and unveil elements hidden in our being. It is of particular help to those just awakening, or ready to awaken to the realities of God's Kingdom, and their place in it.

In her book, Lonzine offers herself as a guide and counselor, presenting honest, raw detail of her feelings and understanding as she awakened to the reality of her sonship and citizenship – something her readers can relate to. Powerful revelations are commingled with Bible-based methods and strategies to walk in victory, and to navigate the complexities of the unseen realm as the reader discovers and properly aligns with their purpose and God-given vision. Provocative questions stir a hunger and give structure for the pursuit of Kingdom identity.

As a leader, the book helps to identify weaknesses and "disrupters" we may not be aware of, or have simply neglected over the years. We are stronger for addressing such issues. As a pastor and teacher, I would put this book into the hands of those ready to move into a place of healing and stability. I believe it will give them a head start on their personal journey, and the corporate journey to becoming healthy, productive citizens of the Kingdom.

Pastor David T. Braxton
The River Church
Haverhill, MA, USA

FOREWORDS

In the book *Our Quest for Identity*, we are encouraged to focus on the one who was the originator of oral traditions and storytelling, as we respond to *"And God said"* in our quest for identity as sons with a royal mandate to be creators who bring the Kingdom from unseen reality to every area of our lives. Having met Pastor Lonzine through the Love & Unity Movement, I came to realize a fellow leader who had a deep understanding of the Kingdom. After reading her classic book, *Kingdom 101: The Supernatural Reality of Heaven on Earth*, I quickly came to understand that Pastor Lonzine has a deeper grasp of what the Kingdom is all about. In this new book, we are encouraged to take a deeper quest to discover our heavenly identities as sons in the Kingdom of God.

Pastor Lonzine masterfully lays out our royal mandate to be creators who bring the Kingdom from the unseen reality in Heaven to penetrate every area of our lives. We are to be a reflection of Heaven's royal power on earth as we remain aligned to the culture and character of the Kingdom of God. The Lord Jesus is the one and only Door that we can enter in to becoming royal ambassadors. We have delegated dominion power and direction in our assignments to be divine representatives that manifest the reality of Heaven on Earth.

As she beautifully describes, God's original intent for our lives sometimes seems impossible to experience, but we are mandated from our King to be overcomers of all obstacles because of the power of the glorious Gospel of the Kingdom. God's grace and power enable us to know and experience sonship with understanding of how we can act like one. One starting point to practical sonship is the power of our words. Our words can carry us to dominion or prepare us for defeat. Our swords, interestingly, are in our mouths and not just in our hands. The two-edged sword carries on one hand what God says, and on the other side is what we say that lines up with God. In addition to the power of our words, we must understand the importance of our thinking. And as Lonzine points out, we are puppets of the devil if we are double-minded.

As we enter into our own quests for identity, key questions are highlighted that are helpful for us to consider. Questions such as, *Why are we here? What is God's vision? What are we here to overcome?* The answer to these questions will help us understand how to manifest as sons of God on the earth as we are in heaven. Lonzine shares about the difference between the gospel of the Kingdom versus the gospel of Christianity that many times we have all experienced. We have originated in Heaven and should have the mindset of Jesus as true sons who walk in obedience. Lonzine shares that King Jesus is center stage and we are made in His image and likeness to multiply, replenish, subdue, and have dominion.

Let me encourage you to enter into the quest for *your* identity as you glean from the pages of this book. Begin your journey as you bring your story into this important quest. As Lonzine so beautifully shares, put off the old earthly mindset and embrace your new identity as a son who is obedient in the Kingdom of God. You no longer live in darkness or the place called *Crazy*. Lonzine's insights into Mark chapter 5 are helpful for all of us to identify with the man in this story. Have we lost the understanding of our true identity? What is your name? Come on this glorious quest and discover the real you.

Some teachers share good information that is helpful, but Pastor Lonzine shares deep revelation and a true transformation that she has personally experienced. Indeed, we are the *Imago Dei*. We are the hope of Glory found in Colossians. Lord, help us truly be obedient sons walking in the Kingdom. I highly recommend any true emerging sons in the Kingdom to read and share *Our Quest for Identity* with a heart expecting to be conformed and transformed into the image of Jesus Christ.

Thank you, Pastor Lonzine Lee, for your beautiful and unique heavenly insights, as we encounter Jesus in a fresh new way. Thank you for your transparency in sharing your personal stories with such honesty, and helping us understand the difference between being born again and born from above.

Come, join the journey of your true identity as you learn to live from Heaven to Earth, manifesting His glorious light in the midst of darkness.

Apostle Jack Irvin Sr.
Founder of The River Equipping Center
Akron, OH, USA

Our Quest for Identity by Lonzine Lee is a must-read for everyone in all stages of their walk with Christ. Known for her poetic-story-style of writing, Lonzine illustrates the Kingdom of God in a personal development format.

Her self-reflection with her own struggles, pain, and heartaches demonstrates her quest for purpose, placement, and destiny. This simple truth is hidden from so many believers, but is made open and plain for anyone to discover who they are intended to become in God's Kingdom.

Lonzine shows how she overcame and found the Kingdom of God with a divine self-awareness through the sonship with Father, being led daily by the Holy Spirit in an identity with Christ.

FOREWORDS

Find your path to total victory overcoming your past obstacles and discover your future in your *Quest for Identity*.

Paul A. Moore
Author, *Thy Kingdom Come:
A Historical, Cultural, and
Practical Perspective of Kingdom Theology*
Central Florida, USA

Now to the King eternal, immortal, invisible, to God who alone is wise, be honor and glory forever and ever. Amen.

— 1 TIMOTHY 1:17

To my Mom, Apostle, Dr. Bacer J. Baker. I love you and I love being "Bj's" daughter. :)

And in remembrance of my father, Dr. Billy Frank Lee. I love you, Daddy.

About the Kingdom 101 Foundations Series

The five-part Kingdom of God foundational study series is based upon my first book, *Kingdom 101: The Supernatural Reality of Heaven on Earth*. While a few excerpts from that book may turn up as part of the narrative on occasion, the primary intention is to expand upon the original conversations regarding the Kingdom of God.

I daresay that we would be surprised at how often we unknowingly deny evidence of true Kingdom of God power working in and through us. Our goal is to work to remove the familiar layers of complacent physical realm life.

What sets this book series apart from others? One thing is the voice that I use. It's a combination of oral traditions, old world and 21st century storyteller, personal testimonies, scholarly insights, and as for the rest, you the reader get to make that determination. What I can tell you is to expect:

ABOUT THE KINGDOM 101 FOUNDATIONS SERIES

- Transparent, raw, unvarnished testimonies that go from pain to power.
- Questions and insights specifically designed to challenge, confront, edify, encourage, exhort, and bring breakthrough and deliverance to your life.
- Highlighted aspects of the quest for identity depicted in the life of Jesus of Nazareth.
- Vocabulary words, definitions, and spiritual life application excerpts from the forthcoming *Lexicon of Possibilities, Inquiries & Discovery*.
- Appendices with words and explorations.
- A bonus prequel to *Reena's Quest,* part of my upcoming *Spirit Warrior Trilogy* series.

What You Need To Know Before Beginning: To write about a quest for identity, it is necessary that I also embark upon one of my own. Throughout the course of this book, you will come upon personal testimonies that expose imprints of darkness made upon my soul. Although it is never my intention to offend, I did not hold back from speaking the truth about my own past traumas. Possibly your emotions might be triggered in this process, whether from empathy or things that you yourself have witnessed.

I am aware that some aspects of what I share can be viewed as offensive or emotionally upsetting to my readers. I implore you not to turn away, I promise you that the pain in every testimony is highlighted by the victorious breakthrough and/or deliverance obtained through the power of the Kingdom of God. So, if my story happens to strike a chord in

ABOUT THE KINGDOM 101 FOUNDATIONS SERIES

your soul, or shine light upon a deeply-rooted or forgotten memory, you can trust that the Spirit of the Lord will not fail to be your Comforter.

I invite you to persevere and stay with us to the end, where victory and breakthrough also becomes your portion. By the time you complete (and possibly repeat) this journey, expect to obtain a strong recognition and understanding of who and why you are in the earth, according to God.

It is my prayer that you join me in gleaning and applying the principles of the Kingdom of God to either discover and/or truly walk in the royal power He has instilled into His sons. It is further my prayer that as you embark upon *and* complete your part of our joint quest for identity, you will expand in your sphere of Kingdom influence, and lead others to do the same.

ABOUT THE KINGDOM 101 FOUNDATIONS SERIES

Throughout these pages, you'll find chronicles of heavenly encounters, deliverance, breakthroughs, and discoveries that have manifested thus far in my journey. My quest also continues. I am far from finished experiencing these extraordinary occurrences.

My name is Lonzine Lee.
I am a Kingdom scribe, steward, and fellow quester on this God-ordained call to align with the identity He has given us through His Son,
our Lord, Savior and King, Jesus Christ.

It is my divine honor and joy to present to you the inaugural book in the
Kingdom 101 Foundations Series:
Our Quest For Identity.

ORAL TRADITIONS, SAYINGS, AND WRITINGS

I'm a student of everything related to the pursuit of the Kingdom of God, which often leads me beyond the limitations of the earthly **"impossible"** to seek the ***"What If"*** possibilities of His divine ways. As you travel through the pages of this book, never doubt my belief in the integrity of the Word of God. As we progress, regardless of the topic at hand, I'll keep pointing to Heaven, our wonderful Lord, and His Kingdom. Just as Paul wrote in his letter to the church in Corinth,* I'll also strive to make it clear when something isn't a word from the Lord, but an expression of my own God-given ability to share my imaginings through words.

One of the reasons I begin this manuscript with a few words about the ancient art of storytelling is that my writing style is

---

* See 1 Corinthians 7:12.

nontraditional. My passion for ancient and medieval subjects is rooted in a deep appreciation for chivalry, honor, and a sense of purpose. The grandeur of pageantry, the symbolism of banners and heralds, and the sacred vows—all evoke a time when words held immense significance, even leading to the sealing of covenants with blood or breath. This echoes the intensity of the call that compels us to respond to the reality of the Kingdom of God.

As I delve deeper into the origins of the oral tradition of stories and history, I remain enthralled by a profound admiration for the storytelling voice of antiquity—the kind that transmits customs, legends, and wisdom across generations. Day and night, stories were recounted in reverence, humor, and with a strong sense of duty. Legends were heralded in grand hallways, while others shared stories in intimate homes or huts, and still others gathered around firesides to hear tales of wonder beneath the starlit sky. The joy remains constant as I immerse myself in the pageantry, chivalry, and romance of spoken words. Imagine all the stories that were first shared aloud before being immortalized in writing! I smile even as I type this opening. :)

Oral tradition storytelling, the voice of sages, prophets, and faithful scribes, echoes across generations, imparting information and insights from the original voice of the Creator God. Imagine...Moses documented the timeless words, *"And God said...,"* calling forth the image of an

ORAL TRADITIONS, SAYINGS, AND WRITINGS

unfurling Light Scroll, emitting golden sparks that symbolize the genesis of all our past, present, and future stories, each brimming with the possibilities of greatness that already exists beyond the boundaries of time. Even before we are formed, we are known, and I find that gobsmackingly amazing!

As you can see, I don't express myself in the manner of a historian, theologian, or scholar, which makes sense because I'm not part of that esteemed group. And as I'm also not a rabbi, I do not refer to the Jewish Oral Interpretation (Midrashic Tradition) or rabbinic storytelling method. These pages are shaped by the rhythm of oral legacy, woven with the fiber of fire-tested truths and dreams waiting to be fulfilled. The definition of oral traditions that I use is in part derived from the Latin *tradere* meaning "to hand over" or "to transmit," and refers to the living art of storytelling, preserving wisdom and truth by voice before ink. In the Kingdom of God, it becomes more than cultural—it's covenantal, and current. Meaning, it is entirely possible for us to move from the Medieval to the Matrix within just a moment's notice.

I am an oral traditions storyteller, a twenty-first century Kingdom scribe, somewhat like an intrepid reporter, or better yet, a modern-day bard, poetic storyteller, and Bible teacher chosen by my King as one that writes His Kingdom resurrection life stories of origin, reality, redemption, restoration, miracles, and transformation. It just so happens that I also get to infuse the stories with eyewitness accounts of some of the incredible occurrences He allows me to see. Golden nuggets of parables, posits, and possibilities are whispered into my ear from the oracle of Heaven, and because I believe the message is not merely taught—but also imparted, I write in a lyrical, ofttimes alliterative cadence of imaginative legacy. That means that even when my fingers type on the keyboard, they only form the words, pictures, and phrases given to me by the Originator of our stories.

In this moment, I simply want to honor the voices of the storytellers of old, those faithful men and women that heard and audibly released what was foretold, but yet to be written upon scrolls that could be seen. This is the flow of the oral tradition storytelling that has sparked my life, my learning, imagination, language, and of course, this *Quest for Identity*.

And so we begin.

PART ONE
LOOKING IN THE MIRROR

CHAPTER 1
THE PURPOSE OF IDENTITY

> Everyone who realizes their association in him, convinced that he is their original life and that his name defines them, God gives the assurance that they are indeed his offspring, begotten of him; he sanctions the legitimacy of their sonship.
>
> — JOHN 1:12 MIRROR

This book consistently emphasizes the good news of God's Kingdom, highlighting the Lord Jesus Christ as the *only* Door by which we can enter into the Kingdom and sonship. Jesus is our gateway to identity recognition, granting us entrance to our salvation, eternal life, resurrection power, dominion, authority, and to the Father. He is the embodiment of God's original intention for humanity, being both God's only *and* first begotten Son—which makes Him the supreme example of manifested sonship. And with that being said, we'll begin by clarifying what we mean by our identity, the purpose of our quest, and a working definition of the Kingdom of God that we belong to.

Before Earth's cycles of time began, God already knew us. It's safe to say that His original intent for humanity on Earth was expressed before our origins were ever made known. According to God's word, our identity is woven into His purpose for our creation. Every word and created thing He brings forth is intentional, thus we know that God had a plan in motion before He ever spoke His first recorded words, *"Light, come forth."*[1] Read the Genesis account of Creation, and you can sense the sizzling currents of excitement in that moment of anticipation, when those well-known words, *"Let Us make man...."* were released according to God's intention. He so wanted us here.

IDENTITY (n.)

The distinguishing character or personality
of an individual; the condition of being the same
with something described or asserted; sameness of
essential or generic character in different instances;
sameness in all that constitutes the objective
reality of a thing: oneness.

Etymology: Middle French *identité*, from Late Latin
identitat-, identitas, literally, same and same.[2]

THE PURPOSE OF IDENTITY

WE ARE SPIRIT BEINGS, CREATED BY GOD. WHAT distinguishes us from other parts of His creation is that we are spirits living in human bodies designed for the earth. Elohim, the Creator God gave us a mandate that positioned us with royal authority over the other elements, entities, and creations that He spoke into existence. The Bible tells us that God spent time with Adam, and they communicated with one another.

Have you ever wondered what language they spoke? I believe it was a Spirit language of Heavenly origin, since everything originates from within God. At any rate, we can be sure that they communicated as Spirit to spirit, Father to son, *Same and same.* The Bible makes our origin clear, thus, our quest is not a search or journey to discover *what* or *who* we are. Instead, our focus is on learning how to answer the question that has kept creation waiting for centuries. *How do we truly manifest our sonship identity?* How can we flow continually in the expressions of God's heart released to and through us? You may or may not remember that you are a spirit, housed in a divinely designed body—formed, fashioned, and made with intention. Embedded in your design is a royal mandate:

- to be creative and successful,
- to expand vision and enlarge territory,
- to bring forth from the unseen realm everything needed to refresh and replenish the environments around you,

- to exercise Heaven's royal power—so that the earth and all of creation remain in alignment with the culture of the Kingdom of God.[3]

The spirit sons of God are to look at life on Earth from His Kingdom perspective. We know that we are created and made in the image and likeness of His Son, Jesus Christ, but again, part of our quest is to learn how to make it so in this earthly realm. We are mandated to live differently from our secular human counterparts. As sons of God, being born from above is not about a church or denominational affiliation. We are sourced from Heaven's bounty to actualize the culture and ways of God's Kingdom on this colony called Earth. Our challenge has been to understand how to consistently manifest what we have been deployed here to manifest. Remember?

Kingdom of God (n.)

God's reign, His rule, His sovereignty.
His kingship, His rule, His authority.[4]

AS ROYAL AMBASSADORS, WE ARE KINGS AND PRIESTS unto God, meant to reign—legislate and regulate the ways of Heaven—on the earth, under the auspices of Heaven's divine direction. Graced with delegated dominion power, we have been given the assignment to be Kingdom influencers—divine

THE PURPOSE OF IDENTITY

representatives that manifest the reality of Heaven's governing culture on earth.

Now, I must qualify the previous statements to make it clear that this specific identity pertains *only* to those that have qualified to receive, by choosing to be obedient sons fashioned in the image of our Lord, Savior, and Owner—Jesus Christ. That means that Heaven's Ambassador, the Holy Spirit now occupies and governs you. If you cannot confess this as your truth, or your life has not changed beyond your claim to be "born again," I am going to give you the words to pray before we go any further.

You may have joined a church or done some of the other works that Christian people do. But, according to the word of God, none of our good works count as "salvation points" that lead to eternal life in His Kingdom. If you're not sure, or you have never gone through the Door, then, as an ambassador of the Kingdom of God, I am authorized and honored to assist you. This is easily done. Your eternity in Christ and Kingdom sonship begins with the words found in Romans 10:9-10, 13.

> "If you confess with your mouth, 'Jesus is Lord,' and believe in your heart that God raised Him from the dead, you will be saved. For with the heart man believes unto righteousness, and with the mouth confession is made unto salvation. For whosoever shall call upon the Name of the Lord shall be saved."

Here's what you might want to say out loud:

> *"Just as it's written, I now say with my mouth: Jesus, You are Lord. I believe in my heart that God raised You from the dead. My heart believes in Your righteousness. My mouth confesses my desire for Your salvation. I am calling on Your Name, Lord. As my first act of faith, I boldly state that based upon Your Word, by my confession and belief, I am saved. I am healed. I am forgiven. I am born from above. I have been adopted as a son of God. Heavenly Father, I know that I am now one of Yours."*

Just like that, you have been transferred out of the darkness and into His Light. And may I tell you something else? Your born anew spirit now has a seat in the heavenlies in Christ Jesus. Let's go a little farther in this. Your first gift from the King is the empowerment to speak the spiritual language of the Kingdom. You're going to need to speak with Heaven's vocabulary to truly be effective in your calling. Denominational people sneer at this teaching from time to time, and the struggles they endure prove their ignorance. So let's establish our power, authority, boldness, and joy by being filled up according to the written word of our King Father.

The Bible says, *"...you will receive power when the Holy Spirit has come upon you, and you shall be My witnesses."* It also tells us that the first believers (sons), *"...were all filled with the Holy Spirit, and they spoke the word of God with*

THE PURPOSE OF IDENTITY

boldness." This is found in the book of Acts 1:8, 4:31, and later on in Acts 13:52 we find others that came into the family of God were also, *"filled with joy and with the Holy Spirit."* Let's pray.

> *"Father, I thank you that today is the day that You baptize me with Your Holy Spirit who is within me. I receive the gifts that You release to your own as we believe on the person and name of the Lord Jesus Christ. I want the spirit language that lets me talk to You even when I don't know how to pray. I say yes to being filled spirit, soul, and body with Your Presence. Holy Spirit, I invite You to speak through me. Overflow in me. Rise within me as I praise God. Give me the words to speak, and teach me what You want me to know. I fully expect to speak with other tongues. I will do it now by faith in You. Amen."*

Now, start talking. Your tongue may feel a little strange, as the first foreign-sounding word forms. Open your mouth and release His voice. No fear. Faith and joy are your new lifelong companions.

As you keep praying in the spirit, your next step is to choose to seek the Father-to-son relationship with God that He wants to have with you. And that's what this quest is all about, for us to learn how to always choose to seek and establish God's Kingdom life, in every moment of every day, just as the Bible says in Matthew 6:33 and Luke 12:31. From this point on, we seek to learn how to do everything in life with an eye toward advancing in our identity as obedient, royal sons of God.

Remember how we established that we are spirit beings housed in bodies made for the earth? This is relevant for your understanding. The spirit you has no gender classification, but is assigned to live in a physical body as either male or female, man or woman, boy or girl. A-S-S-I-G-N-E-D. Yes, your gender, skin tone, ethnicity, and so forth is all part of God's desire to manifest His goodness in the earth through you.

So, regardless of the gender of your physical body, you and I are spirit sons of God in Heaven, even while we live as sons or daughters in the physical earth. There is no confusion when you learn to operate from the mind of Christ and think as a spirit being.

It takes a flesh and blood, earthbound, sensually, devilish kind of mind to mess things up. But to manifest the heavenly realities and power that changes nations and destroys the destroyer's works requires a son of God. That's where we come in.

It's time to move forward. And so, onward we go.

CHAPTER 2
WHY A QUEST?

> As for us, we have all of these great witnesses who encircle us like clouds. So we must let go of every wound that has pierced us and the sin we so easily fall into. Then we will be able to run life's marathon race with passion and determination, for the path has been already marked out before us.
>
> — HEBREWS 12:1 TPT

In our quest to manifest as sons of God on Earth, we have an interesting path to travel. Our mission, assignment, and responsibility all connect to how well we learn to overcome or to conquer the cause of the hurts, pains, obstacles, and trauma that hinders us from manifesting our full sonship identity. First, we learn; then, we do.

Did you know that the sins you are so faithful to do are connected to a cause? The Scripture speaks of letting go of every wound that has pierced us, and letting go of the sin we so easily fall into. Meaning that somewhere along the life path we have walked, we connected with various spiritual influences and beliefs about the world that we live in that simply are not true.

Guess what happened? Your journey was hindered. You didn't know there was a spiritual assignment against you--meant to thwart your progress. However, God knew, and His original intent for your life has not faltered. The words that led you astray can be replaced with the words that lead to your victory and success.

What good news that is! It means that the power to change the trajectory of our lives is ours to command. We are anointed by divine appointment to manifest the spiritual sonship power and authority we've been given. As we begin to connect to the grace power specifically assigned to our lives, step-by-step we learn how to demolish every obstacle, and destroy every temptation, controlling spirit, and potential addiction or affliction assigned to thwart us. For a while, it may have looked impossible to overcome. But God gave us a word for that.

In our weakness, we make a stand, choosing the strength of the Kingdom over the ways we have known. We wield the sufficiency of God's grace and strength as a sword, so the weapons meant to defeat us fail repeatedly. We persist in this relentless pursuit of victory, again and again, valiantly determined to triumph as champions of His righteous cause for others. That's part of what creation has been crying out for: ***"Where are you, sons of God? Help!"***

It may sound a little dramatic, but it's a cosmic reality, not just a good preach. The Bible tells us that the apostle Paul saw a vision of a man in the night, standing before him, pleading for him to come to the region of Macedonia to help them.* How much more is the Earth urgently crying out to be delivered from harboring so much evil? Can you hear it calling us? Start listening.

"Sons of God who do the God things in the earth—assemble!"

Marvelous words, indeed. I know. And that brings us to the ongoing theme within this quest. We yearn to be seen as we are known. We seek to **learn how** to answer the cry of those waiting on us. Hasn't that been your heart cry recently? Glory to God—this is soooo cool! The Kingdom is calling. Collectively, we have begun to hear with ears to obey. We have some Kingdom business to take care of—and we are in preparation mode.

Pull out your journal, and write down your thoughts—not what you think you know, but what the Holy Spirit tells you that **you still get to do**.

---

* See Acts 16:6-10.

Our Level One Challenge: Overcome what is assigned to overcome (thwart and hinder) you from breaking forth.

You know that you are a son. But how do you act like one? That is the heart of this identity quest. It's time to look in the mirror of God's Word.

CHAPTER 3
THE WEAPONS OF THEIR WARFARE

"...We represent the authority of the victory of Christ in the spiritual realm. We are positioned there [in Christ]; we confront the mind games and structures of darkness, religious thought patterns, governing and conditioning human behavior."

— EPHESIANS 6:12B, MIRROR

Our Kingdom positioning is not conceptual, it is absolute. But when our mouths contradict the authority we are to wield, we unknowingly speak against our own victory.

OUR QUEST FOR IDENTITY

Here's where we have been out of sync, or tuned into the wrong frequency. The words that we speak are meant to manifest **whatever** it is that **we say**. Think about it. Because words either produce life or death, whenever our conversation aligns with the demonic realm instead of with the Kingdom, we do not produce solutions or breakthrough. In moments where we could have spoken what God has said about us or our circumstances, we did not. We chose to speak according to what other people or circumstances dictated, making the actual words we released from our own mouths the weapons that formed **against, instead of for us**.

> The power of the tongue is life and death—those who love to talk will eat what it produces. —Proverbs 18:21 ISV

I'm referring to the words we've learned to believe and say, based on upbringing, school, work, entertainment, ethnicity, church, and even our social construct. These kind of life experiences have taught us how to formulate erroneous or misdirected expectations in our everyday human life. Our thoughts and beliefs about money, health, chronological age, family, life, and even God are influenced by the secular systems that we live by, which are all out of alignment with Heaven. **Fact:** we could simply take God's word as the truth in all instances.

This weaponizing of our own vocabularies against humanity has been effective for ages, because we either have not known or seriously considered the power we have been given to wield spoken words. God has made it clear that the power of life and death is in our own mouths. Thus, we have spoken words of death to our circumstances. The tendency to yield to demonic suggestions, such as to depend upon yourself or your government, not Jesus, is part of the anti-God culture. Can you see how the earthly, sensual, and demonic earth-rooted mind works against your right to overcome? This is especially true when we don't feel like choosing or obeying God's commands.

> In the message of the incarnation, we have Jesus the Son of God representing mankind in the highest place of spiritual authority. That which God has spoken to us in him is his final word. It is echoed now in our conversation. As High Priest he fully identifies with us in the context of our frail human lives. Having subjected it to close scrutiny, he proved that the human frame was master over sin. His sympathy with us is not to be seen as excusing weaknesses which are the result of a faulty design, but rather as a trophy to mankind. (He is not an example for us but of us.) —Hebrews 4:14-15, Mirror

Simply put, many of us have been seduced into believing that the weakness of our flesh is just another cross to bear. The truth is, our flesh has not been trained by the right master. Jesus said, *A good man brings good things out of the good stored up in his heart, and an evil man brings evil things out of the evil stored up in his heart. For the mouth speaks what the heart is full of* (Luke 6:45 NIV).

Do you ever wonder how our hearts store up good or evil?

King David said, *My tongue shall speak of Your righteousness and praise...all the day long* (Psalm 35:28).

What do *you* say? What does your tongue speak of all day? Every day? The daily act of speaking can either bring forth Kingdom manifestations or cycles of mediocrity. We release from what we've seen, thought, heard, and believe, so we must pay attention to the voice that we allow ourselves to believe. Remember, we speak from the fullness of our hearts, causing the words we carry to either prepare us for defeat—or train us for dominion.

> Let them shout for joy and be glad, Who favor my righteous cause; And let them say continually, "Let the LORD be magnified, Who has pleasure in the prosperity of His servant."
> —Psalm 35:27

Legendary knights of the realm pledged their lives and swords in allegiance to their king—riding into battle, even unto death, for the righteous cause of earthly kingdoms. Their creeds and deeds are epic testimonies of fealty, loyalty, honor, faithfulness, duty, responsibility, and obedience, words that some may find foreign in this modern age. And as victors, these heroic men and women[1] also received the spoils.[2]

As the true sons of God, it is our honor and allegiance to use God's word (the sword of the spirit) to advance the righteous cause of His Kingdom. When we do, we can declare the spoils of victory as ours. In addition to financial forms of prosperity, other rewards are revealed through the ruination of demonic plans, delivering captives from evil across the land and thwarting every attempt to hinder the advancement of the Kingdom. Rebuilding families, healing the nations, and so much more happens as we progress onward in the pleasure of our King.

Our religious minds have been the battleground for many of our failures and defeats, especially when living by thinking patterns that condition us to embrace and believe in our physical and mental limitations. Typically, it is the way that we view God, ourselves, and the satanic influences that distort our ideas and understanding of what it means to live as spirit beings, created in the image and likeness of God. The ways of this world teach us to fear the devil and evil works, leading us to cower in a belief that we are powerless against the devil unless God, in His sovereignty, intervenes to rescue us one day. Where do you think such unbelieving nonsense originates? I assure you, it is not emanating from or associated with the Kingdom of God.

From the traditional Christian perspective, there can be a tendency to view ourselves merely as souls residing in mortal bodies, with lives that accept sickness, disease, poverty, and lack as part of our normal circumstances. Consequently, we often refrain from exploring the avenues that would challenge us to conquer or vanquish these erroneous beliefs. Sometimes, we just fail to insist within our own selves to find out what is true regarding our circumstances or situation. Or when we do learn the truth, we persist in speaking the same lies. For the sake of this quest, we may have to consider the possibility that our own passivity or failure to speak up is what has kept us bound.

Limitations and debilitating diseases are often called our weaknesses, but the truth is that **they only became our weaknesses because we believed** what we were told and spoke it as such. Much of this can be overcome by the power of grace—our ability to think, see, and act according to God's perspective. However, this earthly mindset stems from the way we *learned* to perceive our adversaries—and how we imagined they perceived us.

> And there we saw the giants, the sons of Anak, which come of the giants: and we were in our own sight as grasshoppers, and so we were in their sight. —Numbers 13:33

Sonship identity is not a toggle switch we can turn on and off at will. Our spiritual reality must be real in every circumstance and place we live. **We *are* spirits!** We have souls, and we live on earth in human bodies. Unfortunately, we've spent a lot of time in our minds listening to words that God did not say! Are you a grasshopper or son of God?

To be blunt, we need to realize that we are not the only spirit beings moving about the earth. There are other entities; focused and hostile in nature, actively forming against us. The difference is found in our sonship spiritual assignment, which connects to our designated human dwellings. Our physical bodies (soma), formed *from* the dust of the ground, give us legal citizen rights *on* the earth. The hostile spirits we confront here are for the most part, disembodied. They are not citizens, nor do they have earthly citizenship rights *unless* they are able to inhabit a "host" that will follow their directions, meaning that their influence is parasitic. They feed off of human connections to gain a foothold. These hostile spirits function as influencers—ambassadors of hell. They simultaneously work against *and* deceive humanity, influencing those entrenched in godless belief systems to underwrite their destructive agenda.

Humans are the only living beings that are legal citizens authorized to speak and live on Earth. Those of us who are also born-from-above spirits have been granted legal citizenship in the kingdom of Heaven, authorizing us to speak and live from there, while here. Meaning, not only are we earthly human citizens, but we are spirit sons living on the Earth, filled with God's superior nature.

Hostile spirits have one job: they work to keep us from looking and acting like God. They operate to do what they must to keep God's own creation in a state of separation from His influence, ignorant of what we truly are in Him. This diabolical assignment is one that these malevolent spirits have successfully carried out against mankind over thousands of years. One reason that demonic influence has been so pervasive is that hostile spirits do not ever view themselves as friends to humans. They remain true to their assignment to work against us.

Let me say it again: demons do not become friends with humans—although they will deceive individuals into accepting them as such—which they have done constantly throughout history. This devilish technology (device) has worked well for the demonic realm, since the elementary weapons they use against every one of us are connected to our feelings, emotions, thoughts, beliefs, and words—past, present, and future. In other words, they set you up, get you used to being a certain way or doing certain things against the will of God, and then use what you've done as evidence against you. These connections to our memories of past trauma, future pain, current shame, and other triggers that are linked to self-destructive defaults are typically fueled by spiritual influences that prey upon human emotions. Here's the thing: emotional expressions such as stubbornness, bitterness, anger, self-pity, unforgiveness, entitlement, and pride—are soul devourers—all part of the satanic arsenal.

I'm not suggesting that there's a demon lurking behind every tree or beneath every rock. However, a spiritual algorithm, activated by our spoken words, exists for every concept that you and I possess. Some of our emotions are linked to adversarial spirit assignments—influences that are quite ancient—they've merely been dormant in your thoughts until you appear to be on the brink of liberation. This is when the diabolical order to retain you within the confines of the gate at all costs triggers an alarm.

Our so-called "addictions" to things like food, alcohol, drugs, sex, overspending, gambling, and so forth can actually be outward displays of our inward ignorance of how things work in the spirit realm around us. We flit back and forth between our *"I'm more than a conqueror!"* and *"Help me, Jesus! The devil is keeping me fat, sick, or broke"* confessions, but we don't see the puppeteer manipulation of our souls. We've grown used to being of two minds according to how we feel—because until recently, we appear to have refused to take this thing seriously. There is a pervasive attitude of entitlement in the lists of the "born again," and it sets us up for painful falls.

Am I suggesting that we Christians think we're superior to everyone else in the world? Yes, sometimes we do think so, or at least that's how we come across. And that judgmental hypocrisy has been used against us—because pride is a weapon of demonic warfare. And unfortunately, some that will dare to get indignant over my "lack of love" and my [perceived] harsh delivery while reading these words is laughable, but not at all funny. Do you know what really is harsh? It is the moment that we each realize how we have been so connected to the flawed logic of lawless spirits that we don't recognize how they conspire to influence us to protect their "right" to destroy *our* lives. God did not give demonic spirits any rights to exalt themselves over His Kingdom. So why do we treat these spirits as though He has?

It's not funny until we're on the other side of it, and we do have to cross over to the Kingdom side, away from this madness. To be of two-minds is to permit one too many to have a voice. Some of us need to know that to be double-minded is to be seen as the devil's puppet (I could have said this a lot rougher. If you know, you know).

How familiar are you with the concept of human limitations?

Well, that's where our sense of victimization is rooted—inside a belief that as humans, our flesh (sarx) renders us incapable of being stronger than our weaknesses. The truth is that all of this is merely a part of the numerous spiritually-driven attacks on the human soul—not just our mind, will, and emotions. We're talking about our tri-conscious being (including subconscious and unconscious minds) and the subbasement of our souls, the place where dormant thoughts and unsettled issues rest.

> In biblical Greek, "sarx" is commonly translated as flesh. However, this translation requires a bit more nuance. Sarx should be better understood as mortal flesh – referring specifically to our fallen human condition. Sarx refers not necessarily to the physical needs and desires of the body, **but to the kind of selfish acts they can lead to if left unchecked**...In biblical thought, humanity was created with a body (soma) untainted by sarx.... Christians are called to challenge the desires of the sarx and live according to the Spirit.³

Remember this: Jesus lived in a body (soma), covered with flesh (sarx), yet without sin. He demonstrated the power of a Holy Spirit-led life of obedience. The ability to walk in this flesh according to the Spirit is ours. We do it as spirits, those that He gave a new law to follow, the law of the Spirit of life in Christ Jesus. We've been made free from the law of sin and death, thus making it clear that we are carriers of the power that enables us to break through and overcome every temptation, addiction, and lifestyle of self-destruction.* Make note of this truth, it is a prominent aspect of our sonship identity.

Before we move on, I want to make something clear. Please understand that at no time are you being ridiculed, mocked, scorned, or regarded as an object of contempt or inferiority. If you've ever engaged in strategic activities such as playing interactive video games, studying chess, competing in sports, or taking martial arts classes, you're aware that success begins at the lowest rung. Initially, you have a basic set of instructions and limited resources to perform. As you progress, your skills, understanding, and strategic abilities expand through learning to overcome obstacles, one level at a time.

And if you're one that is reading this, and has believed that our situations in life are all to be blamed on the devil, this is your moment to rethink that notion. What we are doing here is bringing to the forefront the beliefs that have, until now, been successful at hindering our manifestation process. Trust me, I have some testimonies that have supported those lies over and again. I've heard more than one preacher say

---

* See Romans 8:1-3.

something along the lines of this truth: **Either we expose the sin in our lives, or it will expose us**.

We're operating at **Level One** throughout this quest challenge. And that's where you or I will remain, unless there is willingness to pull the lid off of the adversary's hidden weapons of warfare—the strategies formed against our humanity. So let's expose it—for real. Not with excuses. Not with pity. But **with the power of the Spirit of Truth who makes us free!**

CHAPTER 4
WE MUST NEEDS ASK

"...Ask and it shall be given you; seek and you shall find; knock and it shall be opened for you...Everyone who asks will receive, and whoever searches will find and whoever knocks, the door will be opened!"

— LUKE 11:9-10 MIRROR

I am known in various circles as one who likes to ask questions. If making queries is not something that you enjoy, you won't get very far with your quest, because you will have to ask, "Lord, how can I change things to learn how to be a true spirit-son?" This one question will lead to activations of change, frequently involving more questions as you follow a sequence of steps or tasks to manifest His will for your life. Remember, it's "***Thy kingdom come, Thy will be done.***"

Every Quest Begins With A Question. This statement became my posit to define a *quest*. I see a **quest** as "*a question, an internal decision to take a different stance from the norm, to challenge the passive acceptance of a powerless existence or life.*" This definition generally aligns with logical and linguistic concepts, though definitions for the word ***quest***—noun, verb transitive, and verb intransitive—rarely connect it to ***question***, despite their etymological relationship.

Webster's 1828 Dictionary had some relevant definitions, but they were marked as unused. I was inspired by my mother's own dictionary project, so when I couldn't find a lexicon definition that accurately represented my perspective, I expanded the definition. As more word connotations came forth, I realized the opportunity to create a lexicon specifically designed to define these lovely, Holy Spirit-inspired word teachings. I call it "*The Lexicon of Possibilities, Inquiries, and Discovery.*"*

QUEST (n.)

1. To ask specific questions in fulfillment of a royal summons. The journey untaken to find the answers and solutions that manifest Heaven's solutions on

---

* See Appendix A.

Earth. To seek to find and accomplish the desires of our King.

2. A journey or pursuit driven by an initial question, undertaken to seek, discover, or fulfill a goal, calling, unresolved inquiry, or true identity. *Example: My quest for identity begins with a single question—what do I need to do to manifest as a true mature son?*

3. A Kingdom of God query or sacred search that begins when a *"What if question"* merges with heavenly finished realm possibilities in the act of searching or investigating. Typically in response to curiosity, doubt, or the pursuit of deeper understanding sought from the council of the Holy Spirit.

AS LEGAL CITIZENS OF EARTH, WE HAVE VARIOUS identifiers. We are natives of different nations, ethnic groups, tribes, and families. We are recognized and classified based on surnames, skin tones, education, job titles, financial status, age, appearance, reputation, achievements, peers, social standing, and platforms. We are offspring, parents, siblings, spouses, lovers, friends, family, and even enemies in others' eyes. Yet none of those things really speak to the why of our existence. They are merely identifiers—not our actual identity. To paraphrase a few of the identifiers Jesus voiced, *"The Spirit of the Lord has anointed me to preach, to heal, to*

free, and to fulfill all that is written of Me....For this cause came I into the world, to bear witness of the truth."

What about you? Apart from the ***"I am a spirit, an overcomer, a warrior, a believer, a king, a son"*** type confessions and declarations that we might make in the mirror or at church or conference gatherings, can you describe *the "why"* of your sonship identity?

> **Who are you here to be?** You get to find out why Heaven intentionally deployed you to Earth.
>
> **Can you share God's vision for your life in the same manner that Jesus did?** Not what you think it may be, but **the why of what** He has sent you here to do. *"The Spirit of the Lord has anointed me to...fulfill all that is written of me."*
>
> **What spiritual assignments or issues are you deployed to Earth to overcome?** A tremendous clue is found in the things that currently have you in a stranglehold—debt, lack, sickness, offenses, oppression, rejection, unhealed hurts, fear, unforgiveness, betrayal, shattered emotions...and the list goes on.

Consider the dreams, visions, and ideas you've put on the

---

* See Luke 4:18-19, John 18:37.

back burner of your life when life's distractions got in the way. Or, the career you did not pursue because it did not seem feasible. Then there are the "safe" self-protection practices that you adopted in response to the pain, trauma, betrayals, and other negative experiences you encountered. These are the types of experiences and internal decisions that we make that can cause us to live an entirely different (i.e., counterfeit) life—it looks nothing like the life that God designed us to fulfill. As you grow in the realization of your true sonship assignment in Christ, you begin to see which kingdom(s) of this world you are to affect with a release of the grace-power anointing of God's Kingdom.

> "The king is your husband, so do what he desires."
> —Psalm 45:11 CEV

GOD HAS PUT A PORTION OF HIS VISION WITHIN EACH OF us to create the reality of Heaven on Earth. The creative ideas and problem-solving tactics needed to transform neighborhoods, address societal issues, or dismantle corrupt systems lie within the sons of God. By revelation of the Holy Spirit, we receive answers, insights, knowledge, understanding, instructions, and strategies to complete our part in this royal sonship dominion assignment.

The intent of our quest is to challenge the ineffectual ways that we have lived our lives. As we journey through these pages, my prayer is that we identify and expand the specific areas where we have manifested Kingdom realities. I also pray that we fully embrace our Kingdom sonship identity—enabling us to receive and confront the things that have blocked our path. It's time to *"go big,"* and manifest tangible answers to these types of questions:

1. What is the revelation of sonship identity that God has given to you?
2. Who does He say that you are?
3. What counterfeit beliefs in your life have caused you to be out of alignment with the King's desire for your life?
4. How is the Kingdom of God going to be seen through you?
5. What is the one thing you still need to know to fully believe that you'll manifest as a son of God on Earth, just like you are in Heaven?

Let's take a quick quiz. What answers did you think you are supposed to look for? Usually it's stuff like:

a. Healing.
b. Deliverance.
c. Wholeness.
d. Guidance.
e. Change.
f. Knowledge.
g. True Love.

Did you know that when we operate from the Kingdom mindset, we don't need to focus on finding any of those good things? Jesus told His disciples to seek God's Kingdom and His righteousness. He told them that the Father knows what we need, and He will add those things to us. He was speaking of the Kingdom, making His words true for us today. Do you know why? Because anything assigned to us from Heaven is already a part of our sonship identity. Heaven provides the information we need to know how to live as obedient sons of God. We have one source for truth, the Kingdom of our sonship origin. Meaning, we now engage with the Holy Spirit in a different manner from the tired, traditional, "this is how ***I always*** do it" religious Christian style. We're done with that.

> Your preoccupation with your daily needs neutralizes you - it's like you're stuck in midair somewhere! These things are the typical anxieties of every nation on the planet - your Father is affectionately acquainted with you and knows exactly what you need! Much rather pursue the extent of his royal influence and witness how all these things are provided by your Father!
> —Luke 12:29-31 Mirror

Our sonship responsibility is to learn how to keep leaning on the Holy Spirit for guidance. Learning how to avoid unnecessary struggle is as simple as beginning to ask the right questions, stay in alignment, and reap God's intended provision and rewards for His sons. Seem too simple? Let's look at Jesus. Isn't that how He did things? Again, that's the

OUR QUEST FOR IDENTITY

basis of this quest. You should expect to develop and grow in your ability to ask, look, *and* listen for the questions and answers that reveal your unique sonship assignment within the Kingdom of God. Consider this:

An incorrect question will not yield the right wisdom, or the correct answer.

You will not merely ask Him questions, but you'll learn how to bypass the religious *folderol and fiddledeedee** and simply **seek Him for the questions that He wants you to ask**! Then He answers and teaches you what Heaven declares that you need to know to manifest your true sonship.

> For now we see in a mirror, dimly, but then face to face.
> Now I know in part, but then I shall know just as I also
> am known. —1 Corinthians 13:12

Now that you know the purpose of the quest, let's establish just what we are looking for. By clarifying the core aspects of our identity, we will be able to use the ***what*** to frame the beginnings of the other questions that help us complete our challenge: *Where? When? Why? And **HOW**?"*

---

* Although some musical fans will recognize the phrase *folderol and fiddledeedee* from a beloved song, these are actual words from the 18th century. Merriam-Webster.com Dictionary, s.v. "folderol," accessed May 22, 2025, https://www.merriam-webster.com/dictionary/folderol.

Merriam-Webster.com Dictionary, s.v. "fiddledeedee," accessed May 22, 2025, https://www.merriam-webster.com/dictionary/fiddledeedee.

CHAPTER 5
THE CORE ASPECTS OF OUR IDENTITY

> AS FOR US, WE HAVE ALL OF THESE GREAT WITNESSES WHO ENCIRCLE US LIKE CLOUDS. SO WE MUST LET GO OF EVERY WOUND THAT HAS PIERCED US AND THE SIN WE SO EASILY FALL INTO. THEN WE WILL BE ABLE TO RUN LIFE'S MARATHON RACE WITH PASSION AND DETERMINATION, FOR THE PATH HAS BEEN ALREADY MARKED OUT BEFORE US.
>
> — HEBREWS 12:1 TPT

On Earth, believers and followers of Jesus Christ are commonly known as Christians. But do you ever wonder how we are referenced in Heaven? When you consider the fact that Jesus Himself was never a Christian, did not proclaim the gospel of Christianity, and did not tell His disciples to go and make other Christians, doesn't it make you wonder, ***why are we compelled to preach and do something different from what Jesus did?*** Is it possible that many of our own church members, although identifying as Christians, do not know the true gospel message, the one that Jesus actually preached? His message was, is, and will always be the good news of **the Kingdom of God**!

The significance of this cannot be overstated. If we persist in being influenced by a sensual, secularly-shaped religious Christian mindset, we won't be able to fully unleash the divine power of God's Kingdom that emanates from our sonship identity. Why? Because we will remain ensnared in denominational traditions, gender biases, skin-tone prejudices, groupthink dilemmas, global ideologies, and other contemporary controversies that are just as fruitless now as they were during Jesus' time on Earth.

Is Christ divided? No. He is not. Which means that there really is no such thing as an exclusive beige, black, brown, red, white, or yellow church. Ignorance, cloaked in religious tradition, obscured sonship identity, allowing wolves in sheep's clothing to stir up issues of the flesh among us. This allowed the divisive mindset of pagan society to creep in and shape church culture, forming a counterfeit ethnic hierarchy. This counterfeit identity must be removed from within us so that we can influence society and overcome evil with God's goodness.

THE CORE ASPECTS OF OUR IDENTITY

> Now I plead with you, brethren, by the name of our Lord Jesus Christ, that you all speak the same thing, and *that* there be no divisions among you, but *that* you be perfectly joined together in the same mind and in the same judgment. For it has been declared to me concerning you, my brethren,...that there are contentions among you. Now I say this, that each of you says, "I am of Paul," or "I am of Apollos," or "I am of Cephas," or "I am of Christ." Is Christ divided? Was Paul crucified for you? Or were you baptized in the name of Paul? —1 Corinthians 1:10-13

In twenty-first century language, those verses could easily say, *"I am of the democratic or republican or independent party. I am of ethnic identity or social entitlement. I am of the victim's mentality. I am of the orphan spirit,"* and so on. We are exhorted to learn how to live from true understanding of our Kingdom identity, which means spirit-sonship. Of course this requires that we do more than merely acknowledge the various facets of the spiritual identity we have been given to manifest God's Kingdom. The Bible does not provide lessons on how to be "good" Christians. It teaches that we are to be instructed in righteousness, and live fully on Earth according to who God created and deployed us to be.

Some of my favorite gleanings on how to build upon foundational Kingdom of God concepts are taught by ministers I esteem, like my mother, Apostle Dr. Bacer J. Baker, my spiritual father, Apostle Eddie Maestas, Dr. Bill Winston, the late Dr. Myles Munroe, and the late Dr.

Gordon Fee, among others.[1] So, as part of the answer that fulfills our quest, let's establish the parameters of truth. We have begun to see how identity connects to sonship; now let's observe it from another perspective.

FIRST OF ALL, OUR QUEST FOR IDENTITY IS NOT IN TERMS of some kind of philosophical search. God's Word makes His intent for our existence plain.

> Who am I? What am I? When am I?
> Where am I? Why am I? How am I?

Humanity, apart from God's Kingdom, has a counterfeit existence. It is found in the ordinary physical (earth-realm) life, what I refer to as the ESD—the **earthly, sensual, devilish**—systemic mindset. One aspect of that mindset is the constant mental scurrying about in some kind of *"...am I, ...do I"* type of search—even in Christian church circles. These kind of questions are representative of a twisted, counterfeit identity. The problem with the style of those questions is that they cannot be truthfully answered by earthly sources. Why? Because they are counterfeit-identity questions that focus on problems instead of solutions. Our answer is with Kingdom truth that comes from the One known as, **I AM.**

THE CORE ASPECTS OF OUR IDENTITY

> Then God said, "Let us make man in Our image, according to Our likeness..." —Genesis 1:26

Let's turn those "Am I" questions into bold "I am" declarations made by God's spiritual sons.

"I am who... I am what...Now I am...I am seated... Because He said, I am...I can do all things...."

Can you see the difference? In the counterfeit world, the wrong questions are continually asked. In the Kingdom, the correct answers and responses are given through our *"I am"* identity. Here are ten of the various core aspects that shed further light on our Kingdom identification according to the Word of God. Made in the image and likeness of God, we are identified as:

Spirits, Sons, Kingdom Citizens, Ambassadors (Influencers), Heirs and Co-Heirs with Christ, Kings and Royal Priests, One New Man Creations in Christ, Members of the Ecclesia, The Body of Christ, and Saints of God (Set Apart Ones).

Perhaps these descriptors appear overwhelming or like mystical hooey to you. On the one hand, it's understandable, since this describes far more than what the ESD life provides. On the other hand, the fact that our God-designed identity can be perceived as mystical or overwhelming is somewhat problematic. It highlights the adversary's ability to hinder our awareness of sonship authenticity and Kingdom realities.

It is God's will that we learn how to live in the earth as His obedient sons. We are intended to learn, know, and believe the Spirit and the Word of Truth. Further, we are bid to seek His Kingdom, as our only source—to discover how to cultivate Heaven's way of doing things—and thus manifest heavenly life on Earth. In so doing, we do more than discover our unique purpose and life destiny. Another part of our born-from-above process is to receive the fullness of God through sonship identity. Our understanding in this wise needs development. In our quest to manifest as sons of God in the earth, we have an interesting path to travel in the discovery of various aspects of our identity. Let's reiterate this truth: first and foremost, **we are spirits, created in the image and likeness of God.** Until now, the most powerful aspect of our original creation identity has also been the least activated.

I'm so excited! This era restores our ability to know how to be spirits with souls (minds, wills, and emotions). Created in God's image, we live on Earth from God's original intent. As sons, we have the privilege of knowing the Kingdom of God's mysteries. We see beyond human capacity, learning to naturally live the superhuman "on earth" life as spirit sons, citizens, ambassadors, heirs, joint-heirs, kings, priests, new creations, members of the Body (ecclesia), and the set-apart ones. **It's a big "Wow! Hallelujah! Amen!"**

THE CORE ASPECTS OF OUR IDENTITY

GOD INVOLVED HIMSELF IN EVERY SINGLE INTRICATE detail of our divine design. Based on how He expresses Himself, I believe that when God created man, there was light, sound, and a celebratory atmosphere, complete with spirit witnesses to a one-of-a-kind event, the creation of a being made in the image and likeness of God Himself. There is a lot more to those words in Genesis 1:26 for us to learn.

"Let us make man in Our own image and after Our likeness."

This was a declaration! A triumphant release of His own dream for the earth. Yes! We are sons, created in the image of God—the *tselem* and *demut,* the *tsalma*r, or the *Imago Dei.*[2] But His words carry little weight in our spirits if we do not know the majestic power of He Who uttered them. And so, I invite you to consider the vast, endless capacity of the One we refer to as King, the Creator God.

CHAPTER 6
THE KING TAKES CENTER STAGE

In the beginning, God created the heavens and the earth.

— GENESIS 1:1

Many people in the church world (and beyond) have heard the first sentence of the Bible, yet fewer recognize it as God's self-revealing declaration as Creator King. His self-introduction initiates divine creative order—*God exists before there are heavens or an earth.* Through Him comes the initial release of words that not only lead to your spirit existence, but also invite you into the most exhilarating encounters of your life. As we shall see, *every time* the King, *the One who stretches out the heavens,* lays the foundation of the earth, and forms the spirit of man within him, speaks into the earth, *the entrance of His word unfolds melodious algorithmic rays of cascading light.* Before and beyond time and space, waves of sound, vibration, and light collide—indescribable colors streaming with atoms and quarks continuously burst into radiant particles of quantum glory. These are the wondrous elements—the keys to our understanding of His Kingdom.

We commence with the first of three biblical accounts featuring the center-stage entrances of Elohim (Father), Jesus (Son), and Ruach HaKodesh (Holy Spirit) into the earth. Each event demonstrates the exquisite timing, magnificent power, consummate wisdom, and awe-inspiring creativity of the Creator King.

> And the earth was without form and empty. And darkness *was* on the face of the deep. And the Spirit of God moved on the face of the waters.

In the darkness before time began, the stirrings of a symphonic overture commenced as a celestial body became the stage for the execution of Heaven's original intent. With peerless elocution, exquisite choreography and dramatic verve, Elohim reveals Himself as the Supreme Conductor and Producer of *the greatest shows on Earth!*

EARTHLY ORIGINS

> God said, "Let there be light." And there was light!

THE KING TAKES CENTER STAGE

You're seated front row center in a state-of-the-art IMAX 3D or 4DX movie theatre, enveloped in Dolby Atmos® or Sony 360 sound. Your invitation is exclusive—this is no ordinary film. You are an eyewitness to the workings of the timeless realm, present to receive firsthand revelation of the cosmic earth renovation project. This event took place sometime after its original creation, and suddenly, it's more than a screen—you are **inside** the unfolding reality!

Audible sound waves flow over your head, around your body, and under your feet, putting you right into the onscreen story.

> *And the earth came to be formless and empty, and darkness was on the face of the deep.*

The theater dims. Light recedes—slowly at first, then utterly. A tangible weight settles, creeping over your skin. The silence isn't empty; it's thunderous. Pressing. Heavy. Black. **Still.** You crouch lower in your seat, uncomfortable with the unknown. Who knew silence could be so loud?

The atmosphere is relentless. Claustrophobic. The quiet of the theatre is disrupted by involuntary gasps from the people around you. Then, just before sheer panic sets in, your ears are assailed with the welcome sound of softly trickling water. You relax as the slowly streaming liquid calms your racing heart.

Faint at first, the water sounds begin to change tempo. From trickle to stream to graduated intensity, growing louder, an insistent assault on your nerve endings. Then stormy.

Roaring. Tempestuous. Hissing. Powerful cascades of interminable liquid. Crashing breakers splash your senses with an audible stream of thundering, swirling water all around.

You involuntarily flinch as the swooshing sounds create sensation within your body, and watery fingers flick your insides. The claustrophobic feeling intensifies as the darkness —tinged with mists of water—falls upon your skin. It's almost as though there's an invisible set of cold, damp, alien hands reaching for you.

Too overcome by the darkness and the crushing weight to obey the instinct to fight or flight, you remain cowering in your seat. The sensation is awesomely terrifying. Suddenly every fearful fancy you've ever imagined has come together in this one awful moment. Your imagination is in overdrive. Can you still sense your breath? Are your eyes open or closed? You don't know for sure.

Just before you totally lose your sense of control your sharpening senses pick up another sound. *Lub-dub. Lub-dub. Crackle. Pop. Pop. Sizzle. Ba-boom. Hmmm. Hmmm. Hmmm.* A strangely soothing rhythmic purring, whirring, vibrating, turbulent pounding hovers just above your head. And beneath your feet. And on both sides. Now what?

Vibrating rhythms cut through the darkness. Swirling ripples of countermelody shake the gloom with a brooding intensity and heat of its own. Ta Thump. Ta Thump. Whoosh. It almost sounds like a heartbeat. Or Someone releasing a breath.

Comforting. Calming. Steady.

First your heart begins to match the rhythm. Then your blood zings a harmonious song. *What on earth is happening?*

The Spirit of God—Ruach Elohim—moves upon the face of the deep, surging, chaotic water.

Elohim is the focal point for every living creature in His creation. Heaven's inhabitants watch. A joyous gathering of beings' gaze in wonderment of what Elohim is doing. Moving over the mass of water, beyond the commencement of time, times, and half a time, creation and eternal destiny coalesce within Him. He hovers, filling the expanse of earth's darkness with His Existence.

Inestimable beats go by in the hushed theatre. Breath is momentarily suspended.

Then, Elohim speaks. "Light, Be!"

And His dynamic, pulsating, omnipresent existence bursts into radiant view, annihilating darkness in a single triumphant wave of infinite vibration. Incandescent glimmers of joyous fire speedily ignite the universe in endless intergalactic expansion.

Luminous rays of mirthful light blithely gust over and into your body in an endless deluge of electromagnetic power. An involuntary shout erupts from your being as electricity jolts your nerve endings.

Your mind is slammed by a vortex of ultraviolet color and light, while your ear gates thrum to the beat of healing frequencies of indescribable pleasure. Joyous strength and awesome fear of epic proportion shatter your weaknesses with laser light precision.

You break into a head to feet drenching sweat.

Fiery heat courses through your veins in a purifying flood while your heart palpitates at an alarming rate in your chest. As you collapse into uncontrollable laughing, weeping, snotting, and crying; prisms and sparks of peace, joy, and hope fire your synapses. Wow, even your brain feels recharged! Breath swells your lungs until you feel as though you're going to die.

You've never felt so alive!

Then a torrential rain of holy awe, pure love, acceptance and forgiveness cascades over your heart, washing it clean. Amazing. You feel spotless. Unblemished. Refreshed. Renewed. Reborn. Every one of your senses thrums in attune with the encapsulating Presence that awakens all things to a rising degree of expectancy. Onscreen and off. Something *good* has entered the theatre. And you.

Time as you know it is swallowed into a whirlwind of eternal past, present, and future entwined together in a quantum unity of everything, everywhere, at once.

THE KING TAKES CENTER STAGE

What. Just. Happened?

The King has taken center stage.

Elohim Himself just lit up the earth.

Heaven's Light ruptured earth's voided wasteland in an explosion of brightness. Vibrant heat, pure love, endless possibilities, and heavenly blueprints restore the chaotic sphere to the specifications of Divine order as the brilliance of Elohim's countenance shines once again upon the terrain. God's spoken words were released through the glory of Himself to grace the planet with the reentry of His power, majesty, and radiance. All things coalesce to manifest the will of Elohim. All is right again with the earth, as it is in Heaven.

Feel the sigh of relief as the planet breathes the renewed oxygen of the Creator. Thunderous applause, melodic phrases, wind songs, and waves of grateful reverence are released in joyous submission to His healing touch and call to action.

Be fruitful. Multiply. Replenish.

Earth Renovation, Act I. Complete. *And Scene.**

---

* Zechariah 12:1, Genesis 1:2 MKJV, Genesis 1:3 NET, Genesis 1:2a TS 2009.

CHAPTER 7
THE HEART OF THE KING

OBEY GOD'S MESSAGE! DON'T FOOL YOURSELVES BY JUST LISTENING TO IT.

—JAMES 1:22 CEV

Our first glimpse of Kingdom life is revealed in the Garden of Eden, where we see how God, in His delight, prepared the earth for human habitation—furnishing and dressing it with beauty, balance, and provision. He set the sun, moon, and stars in place as a demonstration of His sustaining power. He established Eden to mirror Heaven's pattern. As a colony of Heaven, Earth is meant to be a paradise designed for Kingdom living.

Adam—created male (*zakar*) and female (*nequebah*)—was formed in the **image and likeness** of God and placed in

Eden to rule and have dominion. They were to be on Earth as God is in Heaven. In essence, God released His original intention for humanity on Earth to Adam (the first of his kind).

> *"This is what you [humanity] look like through My eyes. You are ever-increasing. Everything you touch becomes greater than its beginning. You have no lack or scarcity. Every square inch of this earthly territory is under your domain. Your authority and rulership are established well beyond Eden. What I say is what you say. You have within you the ability to complete every task I have assigned. As My representative, everything I have put into your spirit to replicate Heaven's culture is possible to accomplish. I have placed fruitfulness and restorative power within you—everything that you need to exercise dominion over creation is within you. And I am with you to back up the words you release with My response."*

—Genesis 1:26–28, (Author paraphrase)

Be fruitful. Multiply. Replenish. Subdue. Have dominion. These are not poetic flourishes. They are legal decrees, commands, abilities, identifiers, and royal edicts from the King Himself. Each word marks out our authority, our identity, and our uniqueness as image-bearers of the King.* When God made us in His image and likeness, He imparted

---

* See Psalm 8:3-8

more than just His nature and abilities into humanity. Like Him, we have a will, dominion, creativity, and authority. We were created to operate as His obedient agents of change in the earth in a manner that is just like Him. Though Adam's disobedience caused sin to enter the world and broke our access to Kingdom dominion, before the world was ever created, our Creator-King had already prepared the sonship redemptive restoration plan. Yes, even before the foundation of the world, the Lord's own counsel had devised a strategy to restore the Kingdom to its rightful heirs.* Jesus, the express image of the Father, came as **the last Adam,** to seek, save, redeem, and restore what had been lost to us—the Kingdom of God.

In obedience to the Father's love for the world, Jesus walked in Kingdom authority, releasing sonship dominion power back into the earth. He restored access to God's original intent and delegated dominion, identifying us as sons of God in the spirit realm—occupying human bodies on the earth—male and female—created to reflect the Father's image and creative authority in the earth. Because of Jesus, God's covenant word to mankind—and His judgment against the serpent—is permanently recorded in Heaven's archive.† This is why it is possible for the naturally superior reality of the Kingdom of God to manifest through redeemed humanity to once again be in effect—both in Heaven and on the earth.

---

* See Revelation 13:8.
† See Genesis 3:15; Matthew 28:18.

The reality of God's Kingdom is neither trendy nor new, yet there are still many—even within the Body of Christ—who regard the Kingdom message as a secondary notion, a supplemental theological concept to denominational Christianity. But here's the truth: The Kingdom of God is not of Christian origin, an alternative denomination, an invention of the Church or any other religious structure. **God's Kingdom is His kingship, rule, authority, reign, sovereignty—Himself,** showcasing His dominion and preeminence over all existence—visible and invisible, anywhere and everywhere, on earth and beyond. *It is God who stretches out the heavens* like a curtain and spreads them like a tent to dwell in; He sits enthroned above the circle of the earth, and its inhabitants are like grasshoppers beneath His gaze. *His throne is established* in the heavens, and *His Kingdom rules over all. In God Himself are all things held together*, and *by His Word, the unseen governs the seen*—bringing the fullness of His heavenly reign into every realm."[1]

God's Kingdom has a King, subjects, territory, constitution, protocols, and a governing culture. It includes creeds, enforcers, ambassadors, influencers, governance, language, thrones, a royal family, citizens, a military, a commonwealth, colonies, legal systems, legislators, senators, an economy—*everything* that pertains to life and godliness. It transcends religion, is eternal—ruling over all ages and times, **and will never be overthrown.**

THE HEART OF THE KING

Heaven's King is eternal, immortal, invisible—the only wise God. His rule is eternal. Our King meets the needs of His own—even supplying us with the necessary mind that obeys Him in all things. And because He is our Father, He supplies us with training to learn how to operate from that mind so that we think, speak, and exercise dominion as He does—according to the protocols of the Kingdom.*

The more that we undertake our sonship responsibilities, the greater our influence is known in our local, state, national, and global communities. The expansion of Kingdom culture erodes the limitations of worldly systems. By obeying His Word, we manifest His Kingdom.

Now, as the spirit-sons of God, we must unite to manifest Heaven's Kingdom on Earth and image the expression of the King's heart in all realms.

---

* See 1 Timothy 1:17; Revelation 4:8; 1 Corinthians 1:10, 2:16, Philippians 2:5, 1 Peter 1:13, 1 John 5:20.

CHAPTER 8
THE IMAGE & LIKENESS INFLUENCE

Then God said, "Let us make man in Our image, according to Our likeness; let them have dominion over the fish of the sea, over the birds of the air, and over the cattle, over all the earth and over every creeping thing that creeps on the earth." So God created man in His own image; in the image of God He created him; male and female He created them.

— GENESIS 1:26-27

For roughly half of my childhood, my chief influencer was Mrs. Ellen Carter, my Mississippi-born and bred grandmother on my mother's side. A descendant of slaves, my grandmother worked as a domestic outside of the home, meaning she cleaned "white people's" houses. That's how the job was described. Occasionally, she would share stories about the family she worked for, and it boggled my mind that the children of the house she worked in had the temerity to call her by her first name.

Grandmama was a praying woman, and she read her Bible faithfully. She loved Jesus enough to incorporate Him into pretty much every type of conversation we ever had. She made Him part of the family, so I never had a doubt that He is real. But Mrs. Carter was a worrier. She always had something on her mind to fret about. Easy to understand as she grew up in Natchez, in a place and time where relatives, friends, and neighbors were subject to night riders, lynchings, beatings, and other ugly acts perpetuated by the traditionally embedded hatred derived from that era.

I was raised in an atmosphere comprised of belief in the God of the Bible, the reality of Jesus Christ, and societal influences that sent mixed messages about my future prospects. I was both an avid and advanced reader, even winning class mascots for being the highest achiever in spelling and vocabulary. So my grandmother told me to learn how to type. That way I would always have something to fall back on. How true that turned out to be. She also told me I should marry a baseball player because of how much I loved watching the game with her on television, and that I should go on game shows because I scored well playing from the couch. I did neither. Because of her early twentieth-century Mississippi roots, my grandmother's sage counsel never included any suggestions that involved risk. She worried a lot—thus, I became a fearful worrier. Just like her.

My move to live with my mother came suddenly—Friday I was in a northern California junior high school, the following Monday I was enrolled in a southern California middle school. That sudden change fueled a love-hate relationship with my mom that lasted for years. I regarded her more as a rival for my grandmother's affection than as my parent. I admired and feared her, but I did not really know her. And so, I watched her. When she lived in darkness, so did I. And when she chose the salvation that comes from the Kingdom of God, she led me to do the same. She is my biological mother, spiritual father, and apostle. Today, I parallel aspects of my mother's likeness in speech and characteristics so closely that many tell me that I remind them of her. *I am my mother's daughter. When you see me, you see my mother.*

THE IMAGE AND LIKENESS OF GOD IS NOT ROOTED IN OUR physical traits or natural intellect, but in the reality that first and foremost, we are spirits. Humanity was designed by and endowed with God's creative ability to create, govern, speak, and move just like Him. The Garden of Eden incident distorted our understanding of His original intent—marring our vision and perception of who and what we are, as well as Who and where we originate—but it did not erase our image.

OUR QUEST FOR IDENTITY

> For the Son of Man has come to seek and to save that which was lost. —Luke 19:10

Jesus' obedient quest to restore the Kingdom of God is undeniable. Through the righteousness of God's Kingdom, the Son of Man revealed Himself as the very image and likeness of God. And by the power of His sonship, He used the original Kingdom blueprint to restore dominion power into the atmosphere of the earth—specifically to flow upon, into, and through the sons of God. **Image. Likeness. Spirit. Sonship. Identity.** These are the core foundations of our Kingdom-on-earth-as-in-Heaven lives.

> And God said, "Let us make man in our image, after our likeness..." —Genesis 1:26 KJV

According to Jeff Benner's *Ancient Hebrew Lexicon Bible* (AHLB), there are four different Hebrew words that can be translated as image or likeness. We are going to look at three of them, two of which are found in Genesis 1:26: *tselem* (צלם), and *demut* (דמות). The third word for likeness, *demuwth (demuth)* (דְּמוּת), comes from the *Theological Wordbook of the Old Testament* (TWOT).[1]

Tselem (צלם): Image. A shadow, a reflection, an imprint of divine essence.

Dᵉmût, demut (דמות): Derived from the parent root דם

THE IMAGE & LIKENESS INFLUENCE

(dam), meaning blood. This word expresses resemblance, both in appearance and action.

Demuwth (דְּמוּת): Likeness. A resemblance, not just in form, but in operation—the ability to function as God functions.

Imago Dei, Latin for "Image of God," refers to the Genesis 1:26-28 account of humanity's creation as divine image-bearers with the capacity to reflect God's nature, receive His assignments, and manifest His will in the earth. Though the term itself does not appear in the New Testament, it's presence is interwoven in scriptures such as Colossians 3:10 and Hebrews 1:3. From a Kingdom perspective, it describes the spirit-being identity of humanity—formed to reveal, reflect, and govern according to the likeness of the Creator. Further on, the TWOT narrative goes on to explain that rather than diminishing the word 'image,' the word 'likeness' amplifies and specifies its meaning. Man is not just an image but a likeness-image—not simply representative but representational. Man is the visible, corporeal representative of the invisible, bodiless God. So, likeness guarantees that created man is an adequate and faithful representative of God on earth.[2]

> What is man that You think of him, And a son of man that You are concerned about him? —Psalm 8:4 NASB

OUR QUEST FOR IDENTITY

> I will give thanks to You, because I am awesomely and wonderfully made; Wonderful are Your works, And my soul knows it very well. —Psalm 139:14 NASB

The creation of humanity is not a thrown together, whatever-I-can-find cosmic soup. Reading those psalms, we see that there are some amazing truths about our existence: first: that God thinks about and cares for us; second, that He put great thought and care into our formation. His workmanship inspires awe and causes others to rave about His abilities. These truths impact our lives on levels that extend far beyond how many of us currently view our personal worth.

Can you begin to understand why our physical bodies, gender, ethnicity, and skin tones all have a purposeful meaning to God? Do you perceive that allowing the beliefs that stem from bigotry, prejudice, skin-tone separation, ethnic division or cleansing, victim entitlement, hatred, separation tolerance, gender wars, or orphan-spirit syndrome hinders you from taking on and living from your sonship destiny? Our God is intentional in His design of our bodies—He knows exactly what kind of house He desires to dwell in.

Despite the demonic attempts to mar our perfection with ugly thoughts, beliefs, and behaviors, we are all awesomely and wonderfully made to represent the glory of God in the earth! We must humble ourselves to obey Him, to be instructed and led by the Holy Spirit, the one who gives us understanding of our true spiritual origin according to God. Then we get to manifest our original intent sonship identity, in a vast display of marvelous, beautiful humanity. Having said that, it's time to finish my story.

MY MOM, GRANDMOTHER, AND A SCHOOL COUNSELOR ALL told me the same thing: I had what it took to succeed. My middle-school counselor intentionally imparted words of wisdom into my spirit, although I don't know that he was aware of what he was doing. He called me to his office one day for a life-changing conversation, and in a historical season where this type of conversation was not commonly known to happen, the words that this older non-black man spoke to that thirteen-year-old non-white girl still resonate with me. To paraphrase, he said with a smile, *"I believe that you can be anything that you set your mind to being."* I had no grid for "you can be anything," but his words were a prophetic planting in my life. I was only thirteen, but my fractured mind was already set in self-sabotage mode.

My wonder years lacked ambition. I had dreams and imaginations, but few goals. Despite my innate desire for greatness, I developed a victim mentality. Even after being saved, the molestations, rapes, abortion, fears, and other deeply rooted issues persisted. I knew Jesus, but I didn't understand my purpose in Him. I had a church-girl acquaintance with the teachings of being made in God's image and likeness, with Jesus as His perfect image. Sure, I had heard about/read about it, but if I ever even prayed such a thing, it did not resonate as an established truth within me.

According to the what and how of my beliefs, the untwisted DNA markers of my Kingdom identity were not to be found in my own self-expressed image. God's heavenly truth was not my earth reality.

Throughout our lives, people paint word pictures, develop systems, cultural influences, or ethnic markers designed to categorize or pigeonhole us. Limitations rooted in fear or genetics get passed on through generations. We always have a choice to refuse these fear-laced images, but some find it easier to just stay in the perceived image and likeness of past generations. Wounds can train us to identify with failure, rejection, misery, being fat, skinny, ugly or stupid. After receiving ugly image creating words from others, as wounded souls we stand in front of a mirror and repeat those same disparaging words to our own faces, until we start to see ourselves looking just like what someone else's words said we are. As soon as we accept these images, likenesses, and cruel lies as our truth, they become effective in the devaluation of our existence.

Over time, our beliefs and the root basis for our behavior is sourced from the opinions of other people. It's diabolical how our lives can diminish in the darkness of a counterfeit existence, until we shrink and shy away from our own God-ordained potential for greatness. That's when the unhealed hurt mutation begins to lead us to start acting out the expressed negative expectations of others. It's an alien invasion, relentless in its assault upon our souls. Remember, demonic words against God are designed to wear out the souls of His people.

> **And he shall speak *great* words against the most high, and shall wear out the saints of the most High, and think to change times and laws: and they shall be given into his hand until a time and times and the dividing of time.** —Daniel 7:25 KJV

Think about this. If you are not in the habit of shutting down the voices in your head that disagree with God, then you start to become doubtful, fear-filled, stressed, and tired. We can become so mentally and emotionally exhausted that we allow ourselves to be imprinted with a demonic mark that challenges our true identification of self and our lives. Our answer to, *"Did God really say…?"* becomes, "I'm not sure I hear Him," and we just spiral back down into that counterfeit flesh identity.

Who is this universal *"we"* I'm referring to? I'm referring to people that are tormented by fear, rejection, and the sins of their past, whether saved or sinner. Anyone that has not experienced the eternal power of the Blood of the Lord Jesus Christ is also ignorant of the power that the sons have been given to shut down demonic mind games. Jesus' blood forgave all sin and healed all wounds, while His resurrection life power reveals and raises up the fire of life within us, vitality that is buried under diminishing words and the crushing opinions of others. Regardless of words past, or current opinions, both are lies we chose to believe or were duped into allowing to manifest as truths. Now is the time to regard them all as unsolicited and unnecessary constants in our lives.

PERFECT LOVE HIMSELF CASTS OUT ALL FEAR, ALONG with its torment. I will tell you something else. The Blood of Jesus is stronger than any blood contract or verbal baby dedication to witches, demons, the satan, cults, voodoo priests, or any other form of darkness put upon a young child, or an adult for that matter. It may take a little work, but the supernatural power of Heaven specializes in setting captives free. True Kingdom of God sons are those that know what it means to walk in the image and likeness of Christ. They can help you get free. I mean free the way the Father defines free. Free in thoughts, actions and deeds. It's what we do—help get the captives out of captivity.

I know what I'm talking about. God has a story written about your life, and it does not include you being in shackles for the entirety of your earthly deployment. The good news is that God's original plan is still in effect. He has not forgotten the plans that He made for our lives. Connected with Divine destiny, our identity is solidified through the shed Blood of Jesus. As we intentionally speak the God-breathed words that uncover our hidden selves, the same resurrection power that raised Jesus from the dead is at work within us.

In the Kingdom of God, the words of our Heavenly Father establish identification through His plans for our respective lives. They're recorded in books that He wrote about us.

THE IMAGE & LIKENESS INFLUENCE

Everything we were ever meant to be is redeemed by the Blood of Jesus. We are children and heirs of God, and joint-heirs with Christ. We are the righteousness of God in Him.* Deuteronomy 28 reflects some of the ways that God has blessed us. We are blessed in the city, the field, the womb, in our finances, in our comings and goings, and everything we are called to do. The blessing of the Lord is commanded upon us in our workplaces, our homes, our business endeavors, everything.

> FOR IN HIM WE LIVE AND MOVE AND EXIST.
> —Acts 17:28a NLT

The indwelling Holy Spirit is our spiritual Identification Card. He reveals our identity to us whenever we seek the Kingdom of God to hear from Him. Remember, Holy Spirit comforts, leads and guides into all truth. He is the Spirit of Truth, and He hears and transmits directly from Heaven (John 16:13). No need to look anywhere else. Our identity is found in Him.

Have you ever thought of your life as not just a story, but an epic tale of challenges, triumphs, and heroic victory? Remember, God wrote about you. So, what exploits can be found in the volume of your storybook? You'll find the story of you by looking further in the mirror of His Word.

---

* See Psalm 139:16; Romans 8:17; and 2 Corinthians 5:21.

CHAPTER 9
THE IMAGO DEI: FROM MOSES TO JESUS TO YOU

The oral tradition of image and likeness—divine identity—echoes across ancient civilizations, particularly in Hebrew and early Christian storytelling, where the idea of being created in a divine image is foundational to both Jewish and Christian theology. It is a much more exhaustive study than the surface skimming we're doing here. From the beginning, humanity was designed not only to look like God but to govern as He governs, speak as He speaks, and move as He moves. Looking further at the reality of **image, likeness, and spirit identity**, from a Kingdom theological and spiritual perspective can be a bit disturbing to our traditional Christian understanding.

> "The phrase 'image of God' is not about what makes us human. It is about humanity's unique role in being God's kingly representatives in creation. Once we understand

OUR QUEST FOR IDENTITY

what image of God means in Genesis, we will be in a better position to see how this idea is worked out elsewhere in the Bible."[1] ~ *Peter Enns* ~

Richard Middleton writes about research showing a number of comparative studies of Israel and the ancient Near East (ANE) that cite the royal ideology (*Königsideologie*) of Mesopotamia and Egypt. The basic premise is that kings, and sometimes priests, were appointed as the image or likeness of a particular god. This appointment aligned their function—to represent their designated deity—mediating divine blessing to the earthly realm. Meaning: they were seen or regarded as gods in human form, divine representative images of their gods.[2] Their beliefs legitimized the quasi-divine rule of kings, the visible link between pseudo-divine identity and a system of mythic governance that connected the various gods to royal executions of power. Consider these three scripture references in light of the oral traditions of the ANE royal ideologies.

> **Exodus 5:1** Afterward Moses and Aaron went to Pharaoh and said, "Thus says the LORD, the God of Israel, 'Let my people go, so that they may celebrate a festival to me in the wilderness.'" But Pharaoh said, 'Who is the LORD that I should heed him and let Israel go? I do not know the LORD, and I will not let Israel go.'"

Pharaoh's words to Moses when told that the God of Israel commanded Pharaoh to let His people go indicate a refusal backed by a strong ideology concerning deity. His arrogant refusal implied that he didn't recognize the power of the Hebrew God as a supreme deity with authority over him. He was a king who believed himself to be like a god, and as such denied Moses's request and his God. It had to be especially galling to Pharaoh to hear that the one known as *I AM*, not only demanded the release of the Israelites, but also claimed them as *His* people. This denial of the Hebrew peoples' right to freedom wasn't as much about his lack of familiarity with the name of the LORD, as it was in keeping with Pharaoh's denial of I AM's existence.

> **Exodus 7:1** Moses as a representative of Jehovah God, the existing One. *"The LORD said to Moses, 'See, I have made you like God to Pharaoh, and your brother Aaron shall be your prophet.'"*

It would have been understood by Pharaoh for Moses to bear a godlike presence, he was the earthly representative of an unseen deity. When Moses and Aaron came into the presence of Egypt's king, they were both kingly and priestly in their bearing, not peasants or slaves. So what does it mean in our modern day to be made in the image of God? For some, it's poetic. For others, it's positional. But what if it's also a divine commissioning to mirror Heaven's governance, love, and authority on the earth?

While seeking to understand what being in the image and

likeness of God meant to Jesus, I kept returning to the Latin term *imago Dei*. It was intriguing to observe the diverse ways in which being created in the image of God is taught and comprehended across various religions and denominations. Middleton says that "the *imago Dei* designates the royal office or calling of human beings as God's representatives and agents in the world, granted authorized power to share in God's rule or administration of the earth's resources and creatures."[3] In a future exploration, we will delve further into some of the profound thoughts expressed through the numerous oral interpretations. For now, let us venture on into the stories in the making.

There seem to be multiple explanations among Christians of what it means to be made in God's image and likeness. Some individuals hold profound theological convictions, while others adhere to dichotomous or trichotomous understandings of humanity that parallel spiritual concepts. Notably, the comparisons between humanity and divine are not universally regarded as a plausible reality. In fact, when listening to descriptions of faith and the relationship with God held by many Christians, one **could almost believe that God and His Kingdom are imaged and formed in the likeness of the Church!** This notion potentially explains why the concept of our spirit-son identity can be so easily overlooked. From our current understanding of our Heavenly Father, it should be evident that being made in His image and likeness extends beyond a poetic reference to divine origin—a truth that some may accept immediately, while others may do so later. Prayerfully, this understanding assists us all in our positional and functional blueprint of sonship.

Humanity as created, is not only from God but also for God. We are here to execute His will on the earth. He imaged us with superhuman abilities intended to reflect His divine power, character, and nature. Theologically, *imago Dei* captures the spirit-being identity of mankind. Unlike other creatures, human beings were designed to operate as image-bearers, meaning we are:

1. Reflectors of the One that made us.
2. Receivers of His assigned purposes.
3. Carriers of His words and ways (Spirit to spirit interaction).
4. Agents of manifestation of His divine will (Kingdom influence in the visible realm).

We must look at the Pattern Son to glean a better understanding.

> **John 14:9** Jesus speaking to His disciples about being in the image and likeness of His Father. *"Jesus said to him, 'Have I been with you all this time, Philip, and you still do not know me? Whoever has seen me has seen the Father. How can you say, 'Show us the Father'? Do you not believe that I am in the Father and the Father is in me? The words that I say to you I do not speak on my own; but the Father who dwells in me does his works. Believe me that I am in the Father and*

> *the Father is in me; but if you do not, then believe me because of the works themselves.'*

Jesus, the "expressed image" of the Father, embodied the perfect revelation of *imago Dei* restored (Hebrews 1:3). Everything we are to be as sons of God is found in Jesus' expression of image and likeness. His life on Earth is our divine blueprint—our roadmap. *Imago Dei*, from a Kingdom sonship perspective, could be seen as a Same-same unchangeable identification. As He is, so are we.[*]

Consider the *imago Dei* intention for your life—how the Son's image and likeness is best expressed through you. You've chosen to take God's identification of sonship as truth, which leads you beyond pondering what might be possible in life *"if only...."* Those scenarios must give way to breathing His breath with the assuredness that your ability to live as a son of God, governed by the same Spirit that led Jesus, is the stuff your divinely imparted DNA is made of.

Regardless of the circumstances in which you were born, you—like every human being ever born on this planet—have a God-ordained destiny. The unfortunate reality is that many die without even discovering that sonship is the "why" of their existence. You have the answer to "why," and are meant to live out the answer to every *Who, What, When, Where, and How-to* question you may have about yourself. They are all a part of your story—the one that God already wrote about you.

---

[*] See 1 John 4:17.

THE IMAGO DEI: FROM MOSES TO JESUS TO YOU

WE ARE DEPLOYED INTO THE EARTH TO FULFILL A specific assignment from Heaven. From our very first breath to our last exhalation, our lives are meant to be a marvelous adventure, whereby we each get to discover the plans of God for us. He designed us to go on a quest of discovery to meet, learn, and love Him and others. And the only way that we can fulfill this destiny is through true intimacy with our heavenly Father.

I believe God wants us to pursue intimacy with Him at levels that demolish every vestige of self-imposed or societal-invoked limitations. We can develop a relationship with Him that is so seamless that every connection we ever had with darkness is eliminated. We have been given the opportunity to walk in the Presence of the Almighty, to know Him so that He can reveal the unleashed passion of His heart through us —His joy, love, grace, power, pleasure, desires, and glory for all of humanity. Isn't that your heart's desire? It is His.

The scripture tells us that Christ in us is our hope of glory, meaning Jesus Christ is the fulfillment or reason that we can joyously live in the glorious Presence of God. Before His sacrifice, we had no hope to ever again house God's glory, but because He willingly shed His Blood, we are carriers of the Presence of the Almighty. We are restored to a degree of fellowship and sonship that was ever out of reach until Someone satisfied the legal requirements necessary to redeem our dominion in the earth, taking it away from the serpent.

> In it I became a minister in accordance with the divine stewardship which was entrusted to me for you [as its object and for your benefit], to make the Word of God fully known [among you]—The mystery of which was hidden for ages and generations [from angels and men], but is now revealed to His holy people (the saints), To whom God was pleased to make known how great for the Gentiles are the riches of the glory of this mystery, which is Christ within and among you, the hope of glory [realizing the] glory. —Colossians 1:25-27 AMPC

Our Father has hidden marvelous riches and mysteries in the earth—hidden riches that He wants to reveal to us. God knew that the adversary would unleash death and destruction in the earth, but the remedy to every scenario has been reserved for His offspring to discover. We overcome the evil works of the devil with the good works of the Kingdom of God. We are each created to reign in a specific domain or kingdom of society, yet united in the same Spirit. We are designed to overcome obstacles and spiritual disrupters by the power of God's grace. That is a part of the "have dominion" mandate. And we are to do it according to the knowledge of His Kingdom and resurrected life, **not** from the tree of the knowledge of good and evil. Part of our dominion power is to release God's love to all mankind.

Throughout the ages, the origin of human life has been recounted through oral traditions and legendary storytelling. Every culture, tribe, and language has a vault of stories which, depending upon social class and birth rank, can range from historical and traditional tales about divine creation to epic fantasia that sets humans as gods, and the Creator as a mere peasant fantasy—unnecessary or nonexistent.

In the Ancient Near Eastern kingship narratives, we saw in the account of Moses, Aaron, and Pharaoh that kings in the ancient world were often called the "image" of their gods. We learned of Mesopotamian texts, in which only kings, and sometimes priests were considered divine representatives. But Jesus, the last Adam, never referred to His followers as "Christians"—He referred to them as disciples, friends, and brothers (sons). The book of Revelation tells us we are also named as kings and priests forever.* He constantly challenged the identity framework of His listeners, shifting them from a sin-conscious mindset to a sonship-conscious one.

Because in God's Kingdom, the King of kings **imaged us** as kings and priests, thereby confirming our royal identity as God's sons.

---

* Scriptures: Genesis 1:26–27, Revelation 1:5–6, 5:9–10.

CHAPTER 10
DEPOSING THE COUNTERFEIT IDENTITY

THE LORD THY GOD IN THE MIDST OF THEE IS MIGHTY; HE WILL SAVE.

— ZEPHANIAH 3:17

I can recall numerous Bible discussions where one or more of my contemporaries shared ways they identified with different men and women in the Bible. While I did find some shared characteristics with people like Esther, Ruth, Paul, Mary, Martha, John, and Peter, I didn't relate on the same level as some of my companions. The biblical individual I first identified with is found in Mark 5. This man had an unclean spirit and was tormented by a legion of demons. According to various resources, the Greek word translated as an unclean spirit is a impure, unclean, lewd, foul demon spirit that affects your thoughts and your life.[1] This man, sometimes referred to as the demoniac, spent his nights in the graveyard among the tombs, crying and cutting himself. He was tormented by a legion of 6000-plus devils.

> They came to the other side of the sea, into the country of the Gerasenes. As soon as Yeshua got out of the boat, a man from the graveyard with an unclean spirit met Him. He lived among the tombs, and no one could restrain him anymore, even with a chain. For he had often been bound with shackles and chains, but the chains had been ripped apart by him and the shackles broken. No one was strong enough to tame him. And through it all, night and day, at the graveyard and in the mountains, he kept screaming and gashing himself with stones.
> —Mark 5:1-5 TLV

It's true. The biblical person I recognized myself in was tormented by devils, surrounded by death and dead things, and practiced self-mutilation in obedience to the impure and chaotic thoughts running rampant in his head. I did the same kind of thing in response to the demonic torment going on inside of me. Denial, gluttony, hoarding, lasciviousness, and rage were part of my personal arsenal—massive weapons of self-destruction.

I screamed inwardly while gashing, slashing, and cutting myself with mental tirades of hatred, contempt, and self-pity. The elements of an unwholesome lifestyle powered my physical gashing stones and blades of high-fat, calorie-laden foods, toxic relationships, bitterness, rejection, unforgiveness, out-of-control spending, and a lack of self-awareness. The tombs I lived among were in my head, where I rehearsed memories of past sins, pain, wounds, and trauma. I didn't yet know the full range of kingdom authority and power I had over my own soul.

ANOTHER THING I DEVELOPED WAS AN ABILITY TO escape from my body whenever I felt overwhelmed by pain or sad memories. The initial trigger imprint of sexual molestation was layered in my conscious and subconscious, but it also became secreted deep into my unconscious. Over the years, I gradually grew to be more of an observer, and less of a participant in my own life, watching things happen to me from outside of myself. Because I didn't mature in my ability to experience life, I avoided confrontations, conflict, and adventure. I grew in fear, timidity, and cowardice, which I referred to as being "shy." What I did was to cultivate a prideful attitude of entitlement, which created an internal atmosphere of doom, deceit, and gloom. In this season, I also lacked the ability to engage in true emotions.

Victimized by my own thinking, I became a person of happenstance. Negative things occurred to me often, but I seldom exercised initiative to make anything positive happen. Imagine hating being yourself so much, that you prefer to "think on" a social mask. That's what I did. I found it easier to pretend to be someone else, anyone other than myself. So, I created an imaginary persona, and in the process, became so unrecognizable to my own self that as I grew older, I thought that the façade *was* the true me. In adulthood the counterfeit image first merged with, then eclipsed my identity to the degree that I thought of myself as *"she"* and *"her."* Pronouns. But not in a good way.

I also had different names for each expressed personality, but I kept those to myself. My days and nights often included emotional discomfort, especially after I became born from above. Three voices then spoke to me. God whispered within my heart, the voice of accusation clamored and flailed outside of me, and the voice of my soul echoed whichever one I was attuned to. There were a lot of dark, evil thoughts clamoring for entrance to dominate my mind, but I would not allow myself to let them in. Somehow, I knew that I could not yield to the demand of those thoughts lest I become completely absorbed by self-destruction. Disturbing? Yes. And it was very scary. Even as I write this, I marvel at the goodness and absolute delivering power of God's love, while I dwelled in what I called, **The Place Called Crazy.**

LET'S PAUSE FOR A MOMENT TO TOUCH BRIEFLY ON A major plague affecting today's society. Mental health crisis is no joke. There are many people alive today that can attest to the reality of an on-going battle to keep from going to the place in the mind called "Crazy." Between demonic encounters, hallucinogenic (mind and mood altering) drugs, abuses, terroristic experiences, trauma, acute anxiety, phobias, extreme fear, and more, numerous people in our society fight not to give in to voices of torment. **Even in the**

DEPOSING THE COUNTERFEIT IDENTITY

Body of Christ. Sometimes the demons appear to be winning, and we see the fallout when evil seduces, entices, or breaks down a human mind. Suicides, mass shootings, bombings in public places, snipers on freeways, kidnappings, gang violence, children murdering children or their own parents, and other such ugly occurrences are examples of the fallout. And sometimes, instead of stepping forward, we are duped into becoming anxious of the plight and state of the world, and we start acting just like them.

Although some mental states may be clinically, chemically, or medically induced, I believe that it is plausible that much of what we see happening in this age is a spiritual assignment against us—meaning it can be overthrown. Regardless of man's diagnosis, demonic influences are the devices or weapons in array against us. Attempting to eclipse our sonship identity with orphan or entitled thinking processes, demon spirits are merciless in their attacks upon the unwary. But there is hope! God has provided His people with the authority and means to overcome and recover everything the demonic realm has controlled.

> The weapons of the war we're fighting are not of this world but are powered by God and effective at tearing down the strongholds erected against His truth. We are demolishing arguments and ideas, every high-and-mighty philosophy that pits itself against the knowledge of the one true God. We are taking prisoners of every thought, every emotion, and subduing them into obedience to the Anointed One.
> —2 Corinthians 10:4-5 VOICE

OUR QUEST FOR IDENTITY

DO YOU KNOW WHAT ONE OF WEAKNESSES HAS BEEN? WE often fight alone, or we fight one another, which is truly the wrong battle altogether. To overcome, we must engage the enemy from the position and mindset of victory, exercising the spiritual strategies provided by and with the help of Holy Spirit and the Blood and Mind of Jesus Christ, or the struggle is continual.

> We're not waging war against enemies of flesh and blood alone. No, this fight is against tyrants, against authorities, against supernatural powers and demon princes that slither in the darkness of this world, and against wicked spiritual armies that lurk about in heavenly places.
> —Ephesians 6:12 VOICE

While some in Christianity may be ignorant of this truth, the accuser and his minions no longer have dominion over the earth. Jesus restored our sonship dominion. What the world calls addiction and victimization, the Bible calls the law of sin and death. We are free from this law, but we must remind the adversarial spirits that God's sons are in operation on the earth. We do this by activating the truth within ourselves, as obedient sons of God, living according to the law of the Spirit of Life.

DEPOSING THE COUNTERFEIT IDENTITY

For the law of the Spirit of life in Christ Jesus has set you free from the law of sin and of death. —Romans 8:2 NRSV

I testify that there is a permanent way of escape from the influences of demonic power. The remedy is not manmade. His Name is Jesus. By the crown of thorns that pierced His head at Calvary, He has eternally paid the price for every mental torment and emotional despair humanity will ever encounter. The victory Jesus obtained over death, hell, and the grave grants His Church the authoritative divine power that comes from the Kingdom of God. Meaning, we have what it takes to shut down the operations of lawless, wicked spirits. We just need to learn how to unite together to put it to work. Ultimately, this battle is engaged and won with God's powerful words of light. *Words?* Yes. Words. Would you like for me to explain? Let's return to my testimony, we're getting to the good part, where I am encountered by **The Sane Place.**

LIVING IN TREMENDOUS DREAD OF THE INNER VIOLENCE erupting, I kept tamping down my ugliest emotions. I feared hurting someone other than myself. Occasionally, I leaked and oozed a little of the ugliness onto others with spiteful words and behaviors, but overall, I resisted.

The seething rage, self-destructive torment, and pain I carried inside was somewhat coated with a veneer of civilized behavior. But this ugly inner darkness was always on the lookout for opportunities to wreak havoc and evil within me.

My knowledge of how to release the words that would wrench this evil from me was minute, although increasingly, I fought against those forces. But, whenever I executed my decision to rebel against demonic desires, I paid a price. Rebellion against darkness came with a penalty. Self-mutilation was the price my tormentors exacted for appeasement and to turn down the clamorous voices.

My form of self-mutilation was led by a chief spirit called self-pity. An overindulgence of food resulted in extreme weight gain, giving the tormenting spirits grounds to wound more places in my soul. The fatter my body grew, the uglier I felt, and the more I hid behind the mask of being someone else. I did call upon God, but there wasn't a lot of expectation for help.

Understand, my denominationally trained brain was set to believe that one such as I deserved nothing good from God. I could pray for others, but I didn't have the belief that I had the right to release spiritual power on my own behalf. So, I just kept escaping into phoniness, avoiding my true life. Would I call that an orphan spirit? Sure.

One day, about four years into maintaining the behavior of being a good Christian, I read the *Amplified Bible* version of Mark's gospel, and came upon the words that pierced me right to my soul, and gave me hope.

DEPOSING THE COUNTERFEIT IDENTITY

> They came to Jesus and saw the man who had been demon-possessed sitting down, clothed and in his right mind, the man who had [previously] had the 'legion' [of demons]. —Mark 5:15 AMPC

I felt real tears in my heart. *Right mind?* Was there really such a thing? Was that even possible? I had a frantic need to know how to be *clothed and in my right mind*. That's when I began to realize that I had more fight within me than I even knew about. If what this man of Gadara experienced was something that I could have, then I wanted it. I was desperate, physically tired, and weary of soul. I was ravenously hungry for change, and I was desperate to be clothed and in my right mind.

This verse is the reason that my heart opened to the possibility that **I could** encounter God. And it is why I was willing to accept Him however He wanted to show up. And, as I'll share shortly, it was during a prayer conference hosted by our ministry that I dared to believe that my prayers had been heard.

A FEW THEOLOGICAL/SCHOLARLY COMMENTS ON MARK 5

We're about to delve deeper into the account of the man with the unclean spirit, as told in the gospels of Mark and Luke—two of the three accounts.[1] Before we begin, let's do a brief overview of the backstory, drawing from Craig S. Keener's *IVP Bible Background Commentary: New Testament,* and N.T. Wright's book, *Mark For Everyone.*

Craig S. Keener | Mark 5:1–12
Cultural and Historical Context

5:2 Jewish people considered tombs unclean and a popular haunt for demons. People in many ancient cultures brought offerings for the dead, which might also appeal to these spirits (demons were associated with pagan religion). The time is night (4:35), when evil spirits were thought to exercise the greatest power. Mark thus sets the stage for ancient readers to feel the suspense of the ensuing conflict.

5:3–5 Some pagan worship had involved cutting oneself with stones (1 Kings 18:28), and anthropologists report both self-mortification and supernatural strength in conjunction with some cases indigenously defined as spirit possession in various cultures today.

5:6–8 In ancient magic, practitioners often invoked higher spirits to drive out lower spirits, and the demons here appeal to the only one higher than Jesus to keep Jesus from driving them out: "I adjure you by God" ... This language invokes a curse on Jesus if he does not comply. (Phrases like "I adjure you" and "I know you"—Mark 1:24—appear in ancient magical exorcism texts as self-protective invocations to bind the spiritual opponent.) The attempt at magical self-protection proves powerless against Jesus.

5:9 Identification of spirits' names—or the names by which those spirits could be subdued—was standard in ancient exorcism texts (see ancient magical texts and the *Testament of Solomon*); but this case, where many demons are present, is the only recorded example of Jesus seeking a name, and here he does not seem to use it in the exorcism. A legion (perhaps meant here hyperbolically) included 5,400 to 6,000 troops. This man is therefore hosting a large number of demons; they probably outnumber the pigs (5:13).

5:10 Ancients were familiar with demons pleading for mercy or other concessions when they were about to be

A FEW THEOLOGICAL/SCHOLARLY COMMENTS ON MARK 5

defeated (e.g., 1 *Enoch* 12–14; *Testament of Solomon* 2:6). Perhaps they wish to stay in the area only because of the tombs, but in ancient lore spirits were often associated with particular local areas.

5:11–12 Although Jews lived in the Decapolis, most of its residents were Gentiles. Only Gentiles (or very nonobservant Jews) raised pigs, and Jewish readers would think of pigs as among the most unclean animals—and perhaps thus as obvious hosts of unclean spirits. Ancient (and some modern) exorcists found that demons often asked for concessions if the pressure for them to evacuate their host was becoming too great for them to stay.²

In his book, *Mark For Everyone*, author Tom (N. T.) Wright provides an interesting perspective on Jesus's trip to the other side, bringing out the political symbolism of a land occupied by legions of Romans, sometimes known as pigs, a people gripped externally and internally by Rome's monstrously evil force, and the sea, which was considered to be the place where monsters came from, and graveyards, the place of the dead. It's an interesting study, one he paints as having both big and little pictures, a story within a story. He suggests that there was a deliberate confrontation between Jesus and the oppressive spiritual force, but with an ultimate focus on the restoration of the man. I want to share just a few quotes from his book before we move on.

"The politics of Jesus' day were every bit as complicated as those of our own. After the death of Herod the Great in 4 BC, when the country was divided up between his sons, ...the bit to the south-east, where this story takes place, had never really been Jewish territory. It was called the 'Decapolis,' which means 'Ten Towns,' even though different writers even in the ancient world could never agree which ten they were talking about. In the same way, the **scribes** who copied the manuscripts of Mark couldn't agree about whether this incident took place near Gerasa, Gergasa or Gadara — hence the variations which you'll find in different translations of verse 1."

"...it wasn't Jewish land, and the people weren't Jews. Why, if they had been, would they have been keeping pigs? Everyone knew the Jews regarded them as unclean...graveyards were also considered places of contamination. For a Jew, contact with the dead, or with graves, made you unclean. The man who rushes out to meet Jesus is about as unclean as you could get."

"For the century or so before Jesus' time, the whole area had been overrun by the Romans. The legions had marched in and taken over..."

"The big picture must never exclude the little picture. The focus of Mark's big canvas is on one man in human distress and need, and on Jesus meeting that need and healing that distress."[3]

The imagery drawn from this study portrays human plight

A FEW THEOLOGICAL/SCHOLARLY COMMENTS ON MARK 5

within the vast scope of the big picture—political and religious upheaval. Someone was there who had lost his mind and thus, his identity. The demons had "given him a superhuman strength...but had left him a human wreck: naked, isolated, self-destructive."[4]

Jesus crossed into a region populated mostly by Gentiles. It was noted by pigs, graveyards, tombs, and an unclean man possessed by the unclean spirit ruling the region. So, why did the Holy Spirit send Him there? Is it possible that the one question Jesus asked had nothing to do with gathering demonic intel, but had everything to do with re-establishing a man's identity?

Let's find out.

CHAPTER 11
A SON POWER FLEX

> "The big picture must never exclude the little picture. The focus of Mark's big canvas is on one man in human distress and need, and on Jesus meeting that need and healing that distress."[1]
>
> — N. T. WRIGHT

While reading through the book of Mark a number of weeks ago, my senses were stirred again. I wasn't researching it for this book, it was just part of my daily reading. While I would like to take us through it line by line, I won't be able to do that in this book. I believe that enough material has been provided for you to pursue this further as you choose. Originally I read from my New English Bible (NEB), but we're going to begin with the New King James Version (NKJV).

Then they came to the other side of the sea, to the country of the Gadarenes. And when He had come out of the boat, immediately there met Him out of the tombs a man with an unclean spirit, who had *his* dwelling among the tombs; and no one could bind him, not even with chains, because he had often been bound with shackles and chains. And the chains had been pulled apart by him, and the shackles broken in pieces; neither could anyone tame him. And always, night and day, he was in the mountains and in the tombs, crying out and cutting himself with stones.

When he saw Jesus from afar, he ran and worshiped Him. And he cried out with a loud voice and said, "What have I to do with You, Jesus, Son of the Most High God? I implore You by God that You do not torment me." For He said to him, "Come out of the man, unclean spirit!" Then He asked him, "What *is* your name?" And he answered, saying, "My name *is* Legion; for we are many."

Also he begged Him earnestly that He would not send them out of the country. Now a large herd of swine was feeding there near the mountains. So all the demons begged Him, saying, "Send us to the swine, that we may enter them." And at once Jesus gave them permission. Then the unclean spirits went out and entered the swine (there were about two thousand); and the herd ran violently down the steep place into the sea, and drowned

> in the sea. So those who fed the swine fled, and they told *it* in the city and in the country. And they went out to see what it was that had happened. Then they came to Jesus, and saw the one *who had been* demon-possessed and had the legion, sitting and clothed and in his right mind. And they were afraid." —Mark 5:1-15

I've already mentioned that this man is the first person I read about in the Bible that I found relatable, and not in a great way. It is not possible to recount the number of times I've read this, heard it preached, and even ministered from the text myself. If you have ever worked in a deliverance ministry —or confronted a devil or few—you may have used this passage as a basis for asking demon spirits, *"What is your name?"* After all, that's what Jesus did. **Or did He?**

WHAT I'M ABOUT TO PRESENT IS ORIGINAL TO MY OWN study and personal interest, but I am neither the first nor only individual to question the traditional perspective of this story with a different insight. There are a number of scholars, theologians, preachers, and every day folks that have extensively pored over these passages from various sides, dissecting and examining, then expressing their own educated conclusions. That said, this once tormented man's story has become significant to my personal quest, and possibly could be the same to yours, so I want to look closer at a few things that Mark wrote, this time from the New English

Bible. Our focus moves past the "legion," to shine on Jesus and the man.

> That day, in the evening, He said to them, "Let us cross over to the other side of the lake." —Mark 4:35 NEB

> So they came to the other side of the lake, into the country of the Gerasenes. ²As He stepped ashore, a man possessed by an unclean spirit came up to Him from among the tombs where he had his dwelling... ⁶When he saw Jesus in the distance, he ran and flung himself down before Him, shouting loudly, ⁷"What do you want with me, Jesus, Son of the Most High God? In God's name do not torment me." ⁸(For Jesus was already saying to him, "out, unclean spirit, come out of this man!" ⁹Jesus asked him, "What *is* your name?" "My name is Legion," he said, "there are so many of us." —Mark 5:1-2, 6-9 NEB

That day, as I read through this passage again, I realized two things. First, I noted that Jesus' arrival in that region was apostolic—creating an atmospheric shift of seismic proportions. From the moment that He stepped out of the boat and onto the ground, the spiritual power over the region shifted from the demonic to the Son. Second, I noted that there seemed to be three voices speaking, with one person playing a dual role. Through the lens I used, this encounter appeared to involve Jesus, the man, and the unclean spirit dwelling in him. Here's the breakdown:

Words of Jesus to the spirit: "Out, unclean spirit, come out of this man!"

Actions of the Man: a man possessed by an unclean spirit came up to Him from among the tombs where he had his dwelling… When he saw Jesus in the distance, he ran and flung himself down before Him.

The voice of the spirit coming through the Man (KJV): "What do I have to do with thee, Jesus, *thou* Son of the Most High God? I adjure thee by God, that thou torment me not."

Jesus speaking to the man: What is your name?

The man speaking to Jesus: "My name is Legion."

The voice of the spirit coming through the Man: "There are so many of us."

Consider the following:

1. Jesus did not need to know the name of the unclean spirit. He had already called the spirit out by its classification.
2. God gave naming authority to mankind, not demonic spirits. Heaven does not conform to satanic naming conventions.
3. As soon as Jesus stepped on the ground, the man ran from the tombs to Jesus, bowed down, and worshipped. The man recognized a power stronger than the one that held him.

4. The regional spirits recognized the ruling apostolic shift that overrode their power.
5. Jesus spoke to the man, "What is *your* name?"
6. The man starts to answer, "My name is Legion." This is the only identity he knew.
7. The unclean spirit disrupted their conversation. "We are many."
8. They try and fail to override Jesus' authority. They begged (attempted to negotiate) to be sent into the pigs.
9. The unclean spirit exits. The story continues between Jesus and the man.
10. The man had lost his sense of self, his identity. The only thing he knew how to do was to call himself according to his unclean circumstances.
11. After spending time with Jesus, free of the spirit, he is clothed and in his right mind, with a different outlook on life
12. He is free of fear.

My Posit: What if Jesus' primary purpose in going across the Sea was different from our traditional rhetoric?

Let's take a look at Luke's report of this encounter (Luke 8:26-39). The New English Bible says that when Jesus stepped ashore, He was met by a man from the town who was possessed by devils. It also says that the man had not worn clothes or lived in a house for a long time. No doubt, this man was under demonic influence, and it affected the rest of the region.

A SON POWER FLEX

> "...Many a time it had seized him, and then, for safety's sake, they would secure him with chains and fetters; but each time he broke loose, and with the devil in charge made off to the solitary places." —Luke 8:29 NEB

The people of the town would bind the man with chains and fetters, which he would break loose from, and **with the devil in charge** he would make off to the solitary places. Luke says that when the man saw Jesus he cried out, and fell at his feet (which implies the man wrestling control of his own body). Cried out and shouting are two different words. It says he replied *Legion*, because so many devils had taken possession of him.

Let's look at this from a twenty-first century perspective. Have you ever considered the idea that Jesus, who had not had a whole lot of sleep that night, had just crossed over the Sea of Galilee, no doubt under orders from His Father? While on the boat, He is awakened from a nap to face down a fierce storm with high wind and waves, then deals with His team of fearful men. Finally, they make it to the south-east side. He gets off of the boat, only to be met by a naked, homeless, mentally incapacitated, tormented man that was subject to seizures and self-harm running at Him. And what did He immediately begin to do, even before the man got to Him? He began to speak a royal command, identifying and calling the chief spirit out. You get one, you get all that answer to the name.

It was the devils that lost power. They're the ones that did not want to be banished. The man worshipped, the demons caused a scene, because from the moment that Jesus arrived, there was a shift in spiritual authority, **a flex of Son power**.[2] Through one man, these demons had controlled the atmosphere. And through a Son, the demonic reign ended, and a man's identity is restored. However, the people of that region (the Decapolis, or ten towns) were known to be Gentiles, meaning they were outside of the covenant of God. They were conditioned to the oppression and demonic control, so it is to a certain extent understandable that they would fear what they could not understand. It was frightening to see that this man they were used to seeing under demonic oppression was made whole. How was this possible?

God, being no respecter of persons, sent Jesus to restore a man in an impossible situation to a life of possibilities. Despite what appeared to be a permanent state of chaos, a man with a life that would have forever been hallmarked by the influence of tormenting devils was restored by the power of the Kingdom of God. And all the Son did was to **speak** the **words** the Father gave Him to say.

MY QUESTION: WAS JESUS SENT ON AN APOSTOLIC ASSIGNMENT TO restore and establish the identity of a man that no longer knew who he was? My posit and question are here for your consideration, and possibly to challenge the way that you have been identifying yourself up until now. Let's go back to the man in Gadara once more. He is asked, *What is your name?* The answer is horrible. *My name is Legion.* But what if—just what if—the man wasn't actually giving a name? What if he was admitting something even more heartbreaking? *I don't know who I am.*

See, I realized as I read this, that the point of the story isn't just about casting out an unclean spirit. The "Legion" typically gets most of the attention when preaching this account. But on closer look, it appears to be more of a revelation about how powerful the words of God's Kingdom are, especially when released by His sons. **God's words change matter. They restore identity, and heal those that have been mentally and emotionally tormented.**

What happened to this man isn't far from what we see in the world today. People suffering from cognitive disorders, Alzheimer's, dementia, and schizophrenia all share one common thread: the slow erasure of sanity and self. They struggle with memory, with perception, and even the ability to recall their own names. The same is true for those who have endured emotional trauma—victims of abuse often feel fragmented, as if they exist in broken pieces. Even aging can feel like an erosion of identity, as memories blur and a once-strong sense of self begins to fade.

Quantum physicists describe an interesting circumstance called **superposition**,[3] where quantum particles exist in multiple places at the same time until observed, then collapse into a wave function. Liken that to allowing a series of opinions about who you are to float around in your mind, a series of random thoughts that exist in that place, until you're caught by a certain idea or phrase. That's when your mind focuses on, or chooses to believe one thought in particular. Every other thought collapses into that one idea, and that one focus becomes the name you answer to—even if Heaven never called you by it.

Similar to superposition, **sonship identity remains undefined**, until ***a defining observation of truth*** occurs. If a person is **expected** to be a certain type of individual based on societal, ethnic, educational, or circumstantial assumptions, has a defining observation occurred for them? No, because **the expectation** of others **does not create your identity!** There is more to us than surface assumptions; however, there is also a sometimes overlooked reality. Unless or until we look at ourselves through the mirror of God's Word and see His truth of who we truly are, then apart from a significant emotional, traumatic, or soulish event, our identity remains spiritually undefined.

That leads to another question: What if a person's loss of identity isn't just neurological, a sign of aging, or medically induced? What if identity loss is also spiritual? What if, in some cases, the issue isn't that the brain is failing—but that the person's sense of identity has become spiritually and quantumly collapsed by an observation of themselves or their lives formed from the beliefs or opinions they have nurtured about themselves over the years? We know that secular society is trained to expect age-related cognitive changes, and unfortunately, too many people release words over themselves that are out of alignment with the way God speaks. Phrases like, *I'm going crazy, I must be losing my mind, I'm getting older, You know the memory goes as you get older,* etcetera. And a innumerable amount of Christians use that same kind of language. **But what if you believed that everything God says** about your wholeness and health produces a different outcome in your mind?

The Bible tells us that Caleb and Joshua had a different spirit, and Caleb in particular had a mind that was set on the promises of God. He did not allow himself to disintegrate into hopelessness. He had been given a promise at the age of forty, and had waited forty-five years for it to manifest. At the age of eighty-five, he told Joshua that despite the passage of time, he was ready and able to possess his inheritance. And that's precisely what he did. He didn't think of himself as old and feeble, so he did not act like it. He had a true belief about God's promise and his own identity, and he neither lost nor gave it away.*

Some people may be hidden in plain sight because of fractures in their sense of self. They may be existing in a fragmented or fragile state, hiding from pain or repeat incidents, so by all appearances, or at least in their own minds, they're lost to recognition. Trauma, oppression, deeply buried memories, or affliction are sometimes used to define victims. **But we are not our traumas!** The demonic

---

* See Numbers 13-14, Deuteronomy 1:35-36, Joshua 14-15.

realm specializes in assignments of identity theft and distortion. It creates fragmentation through some form of entrapment, inserting a binding tie to the event, memory, or assault, giving out labels such as victim or rejected in place of a name. Then it uses fear tactics to distort and paralyze a person's thinking process and instincts; **all to cause one to identify with what has happened to them.** According to the demonic influencers, once you get a diagnosis, you're a product of your disease. **That is a lie.**

This is what I believe was happening in Luke 8:30. I don't think this man was telling the Lord his name as much as he was admitting his disconnect with himself. He was so far gone, he could not find his way back home on his own. Demonic replacement words or names that match the circumstances are issued (assigned) to your soul, with orders to identify with the crisis, then self-mutilate with words counterfeit to God's description of you. Once you've identified with the spirit assigned to thwart you, it becomes easier to sit down and prepare for the worst that is sure to come. Finally, you can become so overwhelmed that you default to flight over fight. That is the work of the counterfeit life—give up your hope-filled vision, create, then familiarize yourself with the worst-case expectations.

You might wonder where our sense of self has gone. It lies in the words we choose to shape our minds. Every day, we witness the workings of self-inflicted cultural and societal curses: people deliberately identifying with

A SON POWER FLEX

diseases, diagnoses, delusions, and demonic devices. What follows are not merely examples, they are the diabolical technologies: demonically engineered darts fired upon humanity that, many have unknowingly embraced as truth.

1. My name is Alzheimer's—I don't remember who I am.
2. My name is Dementia—I am lost in my own mind.
3. My name is PTSD—I identify with my trauma.
4. My name is Depression—I am in a dark emotional place.
5. My name is Abuse—I do to myself what has been done to me.
6. My name is Aging—I am fading away.
7. My name is Stupid—I can't do anything right.
8. My name is Paranoia—I hear voices and they're coming for me.
9. My name is Cancer—I am slowly being consumed.
10. My name is Cripple—I'm broken into pieces.
11. My name is Heart Disease — I'm wounded for life.
12. My name is Diabetes — I manage, I monitor, I medicate. But I no longer dream.

You get the idea. ***So, I ask you... What's your name?***

CONSIDER THE POSSIBILITY THAT YOU ARE A SPIRIT ON assignment. Your assignment is to operate from Kingdom sonship grace power to overcome that demonic entity that is assigned to destroy you. If that is so, then shouldn't you view your own circumstances differently? Have you questioned the Holy Spirit to find out which, if not all of these conditions are more than just medical diagnoses. Are some hidden spiritual identity crises assigned to buffet you in a physical manner? We touched on superimposition, now let's briefly look at quantum mechanics research on something quantum physicists refer to as the observer effect—the principle that reality changes when it is observed. Suppose our understanding of sonship identity works the same way, but we have only identified with what we naturally see?

The eyes of the Lord observe us through the lens of truth. He sees solutions, not problems. When God looks or observes, He only sees according to His own words, **never** the words of others. People that are only viewed or seen through the lens of their affliction, addiction, or circumstance have sometimes been lost to their own identity, when the lens they use to see is from an ESD (earthly, sensual, devilish) counterfeit perspective. **What if you chose** to care only about how Heaven sees you, and **God's vision became the only lens** that you looked through?

It's possible that this is why, in Luke 8:35, the next time the people see the man, he is clothed and in his right mind. ***Jesus didn't just cast out demons—He observed that man from the tombs through Heaven's lenses, and in so doing collapsed all false identities and***

reestablished the man's singular, true identity. With words. Learn this Kingdom truth. God does not put sickness or disease on us to teach us anything. Sickness and disease are byproducts of the law of sin and death (see Romans 8:2). Jesus did not go to Calvary to grant the devil continual rights to torment the people of God or those that we lay hands upon. Jesus, the Son of God, flexed His power and released the remedy for all sickness and disease by taking it upon Himself, so that we can live free. Healing and wholeness are reflections of God's love for us. This means that every Kingdom provision and privilege that we have is part of the finished work of the Cross of Jesus Christ.

> I am the LORD, the one that heals you. —Exodus 15:26

Sickness, afflictions, pain, and disease of any kind comes with torment, suffering, despair, and loss is the domain of demons, not God. He has provided a remedy for all sickness, whether physical, emotional or some other type of illness. Crippling disease, cancers, mental torments, and sicknesses that cause people to waste away is evil. God is good. We are called to be rid of the demonic belief system we held as sinners and learn to think differently about the ills that plague us. We must see the works of evil the way that God sees them. The Kingdom point of view is the one that we use. It is written that *Jesus went throughout all of Galilee, teaching in their synagogues, preaching the gospel of the kingdom, and healing every kind of disease and sickness among the people* (Matthew 4:23 NET).

OUR QUEST FOR IDENTITY

Jesus is the cure for *all* mental health issues. He is the First Responder to every mental health or identity crisis. I'm a witness. Sound minds are a hallmark of our true sonship identity. And because Jesus flexed His Sonship power on my behalf, I am now one that is clothed and in my right mind—**permanently**.

CHAPTER 12
THE STORY OF YOU

> Then I said, I read in your book what you wrote about me; so here I am, I have come to fulfill my destiny.
>
> — HEBREWS 10:7 THE MIRROR

As we've journeyed through this book, I've been prompted by the Holy Spirit to share a number of personal stories. Revealing so many details about my own life was not my original plan, but remember, I'm on this quest with you. I am a son of God, and I know that I am a vital part of His Kingdom. Yet, even with this knowledge, I've merely existed in places where I need to manifest, especially where I've lived well below His Kingdom standard.

OUR QUEST FOR IDENTITY

Taking on Heaven's lifestyle is vital for the fulfilling of our overall quest: to live from the reality of our sonship identity. Admittedly, it's one thing to know that there is more to you than what you're being; and an entirely different thing to live *from* this knowledge as your *only* way of life. Something holds us back, but what? Let's look at a few other reasons why we have continued to struggle. I'm pretty sure that most of us have a life story that begins along the following lines:

> We were born into the earth in human bodies that are connected to an ethnic bloodline, skin tone, national origin, and assigned gender. We lived according to the ways of worldly systems, in varying environments, with different types of opportunity or hardship. We grew up in churches, cults, or in the streets. We were loved, adored, venerated, hated, despised, teased, tormented, abused, misused, abandoned, feted, lauded, celebrated, educated, left out, or left alone. We grew up as or turned into beauties or uglies, curvies, skinnies, or fatties, plain-faced, pock-marked, or scarred.
>
> Our family lives were storybook or nightmarish, something in between or something worse. We had mansions, townhomes, apartments, farmhouses, suburban bungalows, tenements, tents, cabins, shacks, street life, trailers, or mobile homes in a good or bad area. There were gangs, drugs, holy rollers, abusers, molesters, thieves, rapes, cops, prisons, church people, alcohol, and on and on and on. Within this, you have told yourself a series of "why" stories that justify

> weakness, pain, entitlement, or whatever. *"This is the reason why I am...always...never...can't,* etcetera." While our lives continued on, we kept our respective stories regarding the precious, horrid, or something in between memories in some part of our minds, our lives went on...*until* we got to the day in which we learned about or were introduced to Jesus.

It's safe to say that most of us, when we met Jesus or prayed a salvation prayer, became "born again Christians" instead of **born-from-above sons**. Instead of stepping into Kingdom sonship, we became indoctrinated into the denomination-of-choice religious system known as Christianity. But most of us have also kept that chest of aforementioned memories as a part of our Christian experience. Sure, we know that since we are in Christ, old things have become new, but that didn't mean that we got rid of the old things. In some areas of our thinking, maybe the "new things" didn't seem necessary, so instead of making room for the Comforter, we held on to what we deemed to be comfortable.*

We were not warned, or did not heed the warning that holding on to lying vanities attached to our emotional response or understanding could be detrimental to our spiritual identity. Even now, it is amazing the number of "Jesus people" that adhere to a tribal mentality that separates

---

* See 2 Corinthians 5:17 and John 14:16.

us instead of aligning with the unity of the faith and knowledge of the Son of God that identifies our sonship. We have religious sectors, with sections, subsections, and other forms of division. In fact, if you query any search engine today about the massive Church divide, you'll find stories along these lines: "Followers of Jesus span the globe. But the global body of more than two billion Christians is separated into thousands of denominations: Baptist, Pentecostal, Presbyterian, Lutheran, Apostolic, Methodist—the list goes on. Estimations show there are more than 200 Christian denominations in the U.S. and a staggering 45,000 globally, according to the Center for the Study of Global Christianity."[1] I think of it as part of an Earthly Sensual Devilish Spiritual System, or ESDSS. Whatever we want to call it, **we cannot call it the Kingdom of God.**

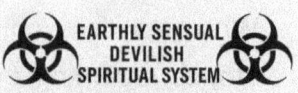

SYSTEM INTERFERENCE FILE: ACCESSED

EARTHLY SENSUAL DEVILISH SPIRITUAL SYSTEM

Sector: ESDSS-1: Religion
Subsection 45-000: Christianity
Subsection 45-000-200: Denominational Doctrine-of-choice
Subsection 45-000-XXX ad infinitum: Ethnic Denominational Segregationist Division

This is somewhat satiric, but also shows how far from true sonship identity the Body of Christ has gone.

And that is why most of us in what is known today as the body of Christ have learned how to be denominational Christians of some sort, **but don't know how to be true spirit sons.** Which tells me that the 45,000-plus Christian denominations and two billion-plus Christians share an undeniable common thread—we still haven't taken hold of our true identity. **There is only one Kingdom of God,** yet the vast majority of us that claim some kind of connection or relationship to Him still need to learn how to be His sons.

According to God's original design, we are on Earth as Heaven's change agents (influencers). So, as our eyes begin to absorb the immeasurable scope of our Creator, we learn to take hold of the knowledge that God really planned our lives for victory. Failure has never been an option in the Kingdom of God, yet failure is an accepted reality on Earth, even among the body of Christ. Father God has no "oops" babies. Our lives are intentional, not part of some theoretical big bang. The creation of humanity sources from the mind of the most focused, intentional, omniscient, omnipotent, omnipresent Person of all times. Can you see that our weak testimony to the world has been our failure to live, move, and manifest our victorious identity as spirit sons in Earth's physical realm?

Now is our time to increase in strength and change the picture that we see. If you can see the weaknesses, look beyond what is in front of your natural vision to until you begin to see the finished work from God's perspective. That is the picture that we are meant to see. In fact, when we view the original intent of our lives from Heaven's perspective, we have what we need to rewrite the story that we've told ourselves for so many years. The good news is, the Holy Spirit, our Helper, is not swayed by what we see. Those man-begotten statistics do not move Him even a little bit. What moves Him is when those of us that know something about how true sonship works, step up and **do the sonship thing** for real. For real.

OKAY. IT IS TIME TO GIVE SOME THOUGHT TO THE ORAL traditions of your life, your true story in the making—the tale that is older than you think. Let's review what you know thus far:

1. Your quest entails gaining a true understanding of your own sonship identity.
2. You are a spirit deployed into the earth.
3. You are born again from above, and are now a son of God.
4. You are a son. You can no longer identify with being an orphan, a bastard, or a victim.

Have your questions while reading mostly been about how do to this sonship thing? Yes? Excellent. Now, this last question is key. Are you willing to forever be: 1) led, and 2) instructed solely by the Holy Spirit, even when...? Wonderful, because legally, you belong to God. Through the Blood price, Jesus became your Lord, Master, *and* Owner. Meaning, submission to the will and ways of Heaven's King is required, not optional. He is the one who reveals your origin according to God. So, if sonship is what you chose to manifest, then part of your recorded story is how you now respond when given the royal command to walk away from your denominational and traditional good [or nominal] Christian upbringing or training.

> "…But seek the Kingdom of God, and all these things shall be added to you." —Luke 12:31

As a true son of God, now you willingly:

1. Allow God to give you the necessary edits for your existing life stories.
2. Give up your "Entitled victim" card.
3. Let go of hatred, resentment, bitterness, and unforgiveness toward those that have wronged you.
4. Cease and desist from finding fault in the way that other people live their lives.
5. Change the way that you use words—give up the mindset of secular society.
6. Give up your own plans for your future to submit to the King's plans for you.
7. Take on the mind of Christ.
8. Let go of the counterfeit mind and lifestyle that you've grown used to.
9. Learn how to manifest the giving and receiving of His love the way He does, unconditionally.
10. And whatever else He tells you to do, do it.

OUR QUEST FOR IDENTITY

BY THE WAY, "YES" IS THE ONLY POSSIBLE ANSWER TO every question. If you felt hesitation or fear, don't fret. We're not done. Let's take a moment to look in the mirror of God's Word. That's where we find our *"How do I..."* answers.

The story God wrote about you is an entire series, filled with words that describe and define your identity assignment. Once upon a time, you allowed others to define you, looking at their distorted reflection of your life *in their* mirror. But now, you know that only God's mirror reflects your true image. So why would you look anywhere else?

Think about it. God's words masterfully sculpt and design us. We are equipped for everything that we will face in life. But the words of this world, rooted in the ESD kingdoms, are like knives that cut and destroy, slowly whittling us down until we're too weak to fight against the weapons that *still will* form against us. We risk losing sight of who we really are when we accept someone else's limitations and fears. Especially during the times that the *someone* is *you*.

Regardless of the circumstances in which we are born, every human being on the planet has a God-ordained destiny. The tragic reality is that many die without ever discovering the *"why"* of their existence. While we yet breathe, our opportunity to find out the "why" of our own lives remains — along with the answers to every **Who, What, When, Where and How-to** question we have. As stated, I've shared a lot of my story in this book. So, let me end this chapter by telling you a bit of *The True Story of YOU*.

THE STORY OF YOU

FROM YOUR VERY FIRST BREATH TO YOUR LAST exhalation, you are on a Kingdom quest. Your life is meant to be a marvelous adventure, whereby you discover the plans of God for your life—and how He wants to affect the lives of others through you. Because your life is not your own, you do not have to be bogged down by the circumstances that come against you. Instead, you rise up and overcome—because your life showcases the impact you have on others. You are necessary to the Kingdom of God—as a matured son, you maximize your strength, acuity, and effectiveness. Father has designed you to go on a journey of discovery with Him—to see yourself in Him and ultimately, see the details of your own story. And when you truly can see the "in Him" son that you are, the fulfillment of His visionary plan for your life unfolds.

You are deployed into the earth to fulfill a specific assignment from Heaven. The only way that you will fulfill your destiny is through true intimacy with our Heavenly Father. It is your honorable privilege to be invited into a life of intimacy with Him, imitating Christ to live from heights that demolish every vestige of self-imposed or societal-invoked limitations. You get to develop a relationship with the Holy Spirit that is so completely one, that every connection you ever had with darkness is eliminated. You beloved, have been given the opportunity to walk in the Presence of the Almighty, to know Him so that He can reveal the unleashed passion of His heart through you— His joy, love, grace, power, pleasure, desires, and glory for all of humanity.

Do you want that? Of course you do. The scripture reveals Christ in you is your expectation of God's expressed glory, meaning Jesus Christ is the fulfillment or reason that you can joyously live in the glorious Presence and goodness of God. Before His sacrifice, you had no hope to ever again house God's goodness, grace, and glory, but because Jesus willingly shed His Blood, you are a true spirit-son carrier of the Presence of the Almighty. You are restored to a degree of fellowship and sonship that was forever out of reach until Someone satisfied the legal requirements necessary to redeem your dominion in the earth away from the serpent.

> I am an administrator in God's economy; my mission is to make his word known to you with utmost clarity. Mankind's most sought after quest, the mystery which has remained elusive and concealed for ages and generations, is now fully realized in our redeemed innocence. Within us, God is delighted to exhibit the priceless treasure of this glorious unveiling of Christ's indwelling in order that every person on the planet, whoever they are, may now come to the greatest discovery of all time and recognize Christ in them as in a mirror. He is the desire of the nations and completes their every expectation.
> —Colossians 1:25-27 Mirror

Your Heavenly Father has hidden marvelous riches and mysteries in the earth, hidden riches that He wants to reveal to and manifest through y-o-u. God knew that the adversary would unleash death and destruction in the earth, but the remedy to every scenario has been reserved for His sons to bring forth. You overcome the evil works of the devil with the good works of the Kingdom of God. You are created to joyously reign in a specific domain. You are here to overcome obstacles and spiritual disrupters by the power of God's grace, and have fun doing it. You get to flex sonship power, just like Jesus did. It's part of your Father and son assignment, part of the **"have dominion"** mandate. And you get to do it according to the knowledge of His Kingdom, *not* the knowledge of good and evil.

God's goodness is not of this world, it is of His glory. You have answers within you that this world needs, and you've been dreaming about them for most of your life. It is your responsibility to get intimate with our Father so that you can learn His heart. Your orders are to become intimate with Jesus so that you can think from His mind. And you must become intimate with Holy Spirit so that He can work through you to manifest the help this world needs from the unseen Heaven into the seen things of Earth. That is part of your dominion power, to release God's love to all mankind.

This, dear friend, is only part of the story of Y-O-U. Every step of your quest, God's divine narrative continues to unfold. Every area where pain, trauma, and emotional distress appear to triumph over you, the Author of your life has already equipped you with everything necessary to rewrite the stories of your days. You are a dearly beloved son of God! Victory is embedded within your spiritual DNA, and God has already declared His intentions concerning you. He believes that His own words about you are the presiding determination over the rest of your story.[2]

So, beloved of God, **Who do you believe?**

PART II
THE POWER OF SONSHIP

CHAPTER 13
MY JESUS ENCOUNTER

BUT WE DO SEE JESUS, WHO WAS MADE LOWER THAN THE ANGELS FOR A LITTLE WHILE, NOW CROWNED WITH GLORY AND HONOR BECAUSE HE SUFFERED DEATH, SO THAT BY THE GRACE OF GOD HE MIGHT TASTE DEATH FOR EVERYONE.

— HEBREWS 2:9 NIV

For about ten or so years, we had a multicultural congregation in San Jose, California called *New Growth*. About five years in, our church held its first—and only—annual conference— in a hotel banquet room in Monterey. Somehow, the familiar ninety-minute drive became a time of confusion. It took four hours to arrive that Friday night. I missed the entire message, by the time I arrived, personal ministry was in full session.

Entering that banquet room turned sanctuary, I was enveloped in a glorious atmosphere. The room was filled with a mix of noise—people weeping, praying, and walking. Worshipping God. Instructed to find a place to pray and seek the Lord, I crawled underneath the nearest table. The moment the cloth dropped behind me, a peaceful hush occurred as if a door had closed, shutting out all the other sounds.

My natural eyes saw no one, yet I sensed His Presence. My spirit leapt in recognition of the One that I belong to. Yes, it was Jesus. JESUS! The Lord Jesus Himself met me under a banquet table in Monterey, California! Everything in my being recognized Him. Oh, what a glorious moment, just being there.

Have you experienced this? Peace flooding through your entire being, an awareness of something greater than your dreams? You want to laugh, cry, bow, fall on your face, surrender, and worship all at the same time. Meanwhile your inner self screams like a teen-age fan girl, *"It's Jesus! It's Jesus!"* When you belong to Him, you just know.

Let me tell you, Love and Acceptance emanate from His being. There is an increase—a rush of emotion, awe, and inner calm that happens. Peace. That's what I felt that night, calm, peaceful, and safe. The commanding force of His being overcame me. Despite all my masks, ugliness, and demonic influences, Jesus came in and claimed me as His. Somehow, I knew that everything would be all right. And then, Jesus spoke, asking what I wanted Him to do...for me.

In answer to His question, I told Him I wanted to be made whole. *"Lord, I want to know what it means to be in my right mind."* It took Him less time to answer than it did for me to make my request. This encounter occurred a number of years ago, but I still remember the miraculous change that began right underneath that table. After I prayed, my spirit eyes opened, and I watched as the floating part of myself returned into my body. Then I felt myself being fused together while the opening was sealed shut.

Did you know that you do not have to be worthy of God's love to be loved? I lacked any sense of worth, yet the love of God healed and delivered me from decades of torment. There was no drama involved. The Master with the key to me entered in and unlocked my shackles. Even though I didn't think I deserved anything good, Jesus showed up, and those tormenting spirits left me. Remember how Jesus spoke to the unclean spirit?

> "…He said to him, 'Come out of the man, unclean spirit!'" —Mark 5:8

That's what happened with me. The "crazy madness" was gone. For the first time in years, I felt like I was just one person. The clamor of the outside voices was rebuked into silence. The demonic ability to escape from my body is gone. Forever. My testimony from that night on is that God heard the cry of His son, **"I want to be in my right mind!"**

That son was me. And Jesus made a house call. Hallelujah!

CHAPTER 14
SPIRITUAL DISRUPTERS

You were running a good race. Who cut in on you to keep you from obeying the truth?

— GALATIANS 5:7

You might be familiar with these sentiments: *"If just looks like the Universe is conspiring against me...I feel like the whole world is out to get me."* These are secular expressions that describe feelings of being targeted by external forces as life consistently goes wrong or obstacles appear at every turn. Some use such words to express the experience of supposed bad luck or misfortune, implying a belief that fate, destiny, or unseen forces are working to hinder progress, personal desires, well-being, or goals. Ever been there?

It is no coincidence that the Holy Spirit began to speak with me concerning what is known as spiritual disrupters. Divine disruption is a spiritual prayer strategy used by us during intercessory prayer. In these moments, we direct our words to stop the influence and plans of wicked spirits, known as heavenly interventions or strategic strikes. We call for the forces of the word of God, angelic assistance, or other Kingdom elements to foil the plans and actions of those opposing our King's will.

> Used as a **noun**, a DISRUPTER is a person or thing that interrupts an event, activity, or process by causing a disturbance or problem. In BIOLOGY: it is a thing that interferes with or significantly alters the structure or function of a biological molecule such as a gene or hormone.[1] SPIRITUALLY speaking: contextual keywords for *disrupter* include: divine intervention, change of frequency, time, or outcome, cosmic alteration, mental assault, demonic interference, traumatic experience, and the effect of spiritual laws, i.e., sin and death, knowledge of good and evil, spirit of life in Christ Jesus.*

As the Holy Spirit spoke to me on this topic, He made it known that His reference was directed toward events in my own life. He specifically referred to the emotional disruptions, hindrances and repetitive cycles of self-sabotage

---

* See Appendix A.

that have been strongholds in certain areas of my thinking, doing, and being. These pertain in part to traumatic incidents that occurred during my childhood. **Please be advised**, this chapter touches on some of the ugliest parts of my life. If your emotions overwhelm you, or my words strike a familiar or painful chord, I pray that you seek out the Holy Spirit, our Comforter, and be inwardly strengthened with His might. Let nothing deter your quest. Every personal experience I share is prompted by the Holy Spirit. No part of my life story is from a victim perspective, but as one who the Son has made free. That freedom is also your portion.

I LEARNED THAT IN CERTAIN AREAS OF MY LIFE, I HAVE operated from a darkened perception of truth. Yes, I grew up in a house with the knowledge of Jesus, had my first baptism experience at the age of nine, a true salvation experience as a young adult, and have the honor to teach and release the message of the Kingdom of God over the years. But I also battled depression, oppression, suicidal notions, torment, unclean thoughts, and self-hatred. Here's how it began.

At the age of eight, I became an unreported statistic of incestuous rape.[2] It occurred during a weekend visit with some distant family members. Awakened from sleep by the pain and shock of invasion, I was catapulted into a flurry of confusion and other unidentified emotions that were too much to bear. Not understanding what was happening, I instinctively withdrew from my present-moment reality. In that instant, the bouncy, bubbly, laugh-filled, joyous little girl disappeared. The first moments of a counterfeit identity, a result of childhood trauma, had just come to me. For years this demonic spiritual disruption would contaminate every aspect of my life—including how I have thought, believed, acted, and reacted to people, circumstances, God, and myself. The perpetrator was safe from exposure because I was too young, innocent, and ashamed to tell what had happened to me.

Through my growing years, young adulthood, marriage, parenthood, ministry, and every other facet of my life, I viewed myself through a pervasive haze of darkness. My identity *was* viewed through eyes of continuance, my mind filled with thoughts twisted in a hapless coil of impossibilities. Far down a tunnel, I could see something amazing, but didn't think I'd ever realize it—that is, not until the day when the Holy Spirit directed me to ask Him a series of questions. Specifically, questions that He wanted to answer, so that His light of Truth could give me the understanding Heaven held in reserve for me.

I still marvel at the difference that Truth makes. The entrance of His Word brought heavenly light to a darkened area of my mind. We will expound upon the entrance of the light of His Word and some of my recent breakthroughs in later chapters. For now, let's establish a scriptural understanding for context concerning these disrupters: how they get in our way, and what their demonic agenda is meant to accomplish.

SPIRITUAL DISRUPTERS

THE FIRST SPIRITUAL DISRUPTION THAT OCCURRED within the span of human existence is seen in Genesis 3:1-7. To gain the full context requires reading and breakdown of the entire chapter. However, we're going to highlight three points from the seventh verse that encapsulates the outcome of the royal couple's encounter with the demonic disrupter in the Garden.

> And **the eyes of them both were opened**, and **they knew** that they *were* **naked**..." Genesis 3:7a [author bold emphasis]

The *Ancient Hebrew Lexicon of the Bible* has an interesting breakdown of the **bolded words** in the scripture above. The King James version says that after eating the fruit from the tree, the eyes of both the man and woman were opened, indicating that the same knowledge came to both of them—they each knew that they were naked.

What did that mean exactly? In ancient Hebrew thought, "opening one's eyes" often symbolizes gaining new understanding, awareness, or discernment. Before eating the fruit, they had no concept of shame, fear, right, wrong—no awareness of ethics or morals; after eating, their eyes were "opened" to the knowledge of good and evil, as described earlier.

Figuratively speaking, the Hebrew word for eyes, עין ('ayin) represents **perception**, not only physical sight but also **spiritual insight**. The pictographs for this word are of an eye and a seed, together defined as the *eye of continuance*. Descriptive terminology depicts the idea of a furrow formed between the eyes when intently looking at something, an affliction, oppression, the look of depression…or a cloud as a covering that provides shade.

The figure of speech used here is referred to as *metonymy of the subject*. This occurs when a word is used to represent something closely related to or caused by it. In the case of the word **"naked,"** a sense of awareness came upon the man and woman after sinning. A cloak of awareness that revealed traumatic devastation, much more than just the literal meaning of being without clothes. E.W. Bullinger makes the point that the royal couple already *knew* what physical nakedness was. After eating the fruit, the concept of nakedness took on a new, shameful meaning because their divine identity had been distorted through the interference of a fallen spirit.[3]

As we read this type of theological interpretation, possible answers to the question of what really happened to the royal couple after this incident start to materialize. As soon as they ate the fruit, they were instantly severed from the mind that enabled intimate fellowship with their Creator God. Further exploration, with a touch of imagination allows the reality of their traumatic peril to resonate with our own human understanding. How did this sudden loss affected their sensory nervous systems? The opening of their eyes was also the darkening of their minds. They were assaulted—mentally and emotionally—by a steady stream of unfamiliar images, soul-jarring sounds, and violent emotions. Knowledge from a lower realm laid claim to their mind, will, and emotions. This was an alien invasion. Guilt, shame, and fear entered their awareness—and life as they knew it was traded away for a tempest of chaos and confusion.

What happened to their sense of security? Their protective light was gone. The cloak of love they had always known was replaced with a shroud of malevolence. Purity and innocence gave way to an awareness of good, evil, right, wrong, and moral consciousness—things they did not even know existed. They had just suffered the loss of the Kingdom of God *and* their royal identity.

They were spiritually disrupted—moved from living according to God's extension of royal power—into a fallen existence. One bite of the fruit with roots planted in the knowledge of good and evil stripped them of divine authority, subjecting them to fear the very things they had been given reign over. They became what they were never created to be; power-stripped, traumatized souls, catapulted out of original design into a lower-realm existence.

CAN YOU IMAGINE THE HORROR OF THAT DAY? *WHAT DO you think* they saw through the eyes of continuance? I believe they saw life through a darkened glass, an earthly reality of life without the fellowship and authoritative power they once had from the Kingdom of God. They saw the price they paid: one decision moved them from alignment with the will of God to subjection to the influence of a fallen spirit. They actually knew what it felt like to be reduced to a merely human identity. Humanity would still continue to be fruitful, multiply, and till the soil of the earth, however they no longer had dominion to subdue it. Deception now clouded truth, and destiny became distorted according to the futility of human understanding. That's what they saw, but I believe they also *heard* with hope what God later spoke.* And they understood—having retained an instinctive awareness of the safety of His love—that this lower human status would not last forever.

> O FOOLISH GALATIANS, WHO HATH BEWITCHED YOU,
> THAT YE SHOULD NOT OBEY THE TRUTH...?
> —Galatians 3:1

IN HIS LETTER TO THE CHURCHES IN GALATIA, PAUL speaks to the outside influences the people of this region faced. The spirit of religion was constantly at work to pull the

---

* See Genesis 3:8-19.

new converts into the traditional ways of Judaism, and to forsake the teachings of Christ. His question, *"Who bewitched you?"* strikes at the heart of the spiritual disruption of that day.

While God has a plan for every single person in creation, the demonic spirits are on assignment to thwart His intention by whatever means necessary. These disrupters come in the form of addictions, sickness and disease, poverty, lack, debt, fear, divorce, trauma, and memories of the past. Within secular society, these patterns and cycles of disaster are commonly referred to as "bad luck" or "karma." However, it's not luck, karma, the world, or the universe. Quite simply, it is spiritual opposition to the workings of God in our lives. The workings of the league of the accuser of the brethren thrives upon the ignorance of humanity. As long as we are willing to simply accept and go along with life as it happens, the truth of our intended identity and purpose in life remains a misty, hazy blur.

Starting out, I did not know how to fight. Acceptance of my circumstances was the fruit of self-protective coping mechanisms and patterns planted in my unconscious and subconscious emotional centers. The little girl that left for the weekend was not the same one that was returned to my grandmother's house. My original expression was lost, which is why I think I kept the rape a secret, telling no one what had happened to me. Truth to tell, I did not know how to articulate such a thing.

Silence was the first result of the criminal invasion of my body. Still innocent in my choices and my understanding, I now had an intimate knowledge of evil. My purity was blighted by a perverse awareness, something that kindled desires that I was far too young to define, let alone have. So with this kind of twisted perspective, it is understandable that my instinct was to hide from the light of truth.

My grandmother was my safe place. I did not really think about being loved by anyone else, not even my mom or God. But, at the age of nine I heard Him call me to Himself. I responded by walking down the church aisle, and becoming a candidate for baptism, and church member. By the time I was around 11 or so, I had rotated back to the counterfeit idea that I was just worthless, damaged goods. In order to cope, I had to develop ways to deal with emotional pain, trauma and stress. So I took on the pretense personality, demeanor, behaviors, speech patterns, and other little habits that would keep me "safe."

The bubbly child became somewhat anxious, quiet and reserved, so much so that my grandmother called me timid. My demeanor was that of an insecure, uncertain, awkward, nervous, and self-conscious little girl—considered quite shy, although at times I could be quite the incessant chatterer. The truth is, I wanted to be invisible, not draw attention to myself. My body was an embarrassment to me because it was the cause of my problems.

SPIRITUAL DISRUPTERS

Food became a comfort, and in some ways, a means to mistreat the body that had caused me so much trouble. I remember thinking that if I was fat, no one would want me. I also remember the many years that I thought of myself as "she" and "her," and when embarrassing, difficult, or frightening situations occurred, I would just detach from what was happening and watch myself from the outside—an involuntary form of astral projection, carried from childhood into adult years.

Some readers may relate to what I'm saying, so you'll understand that I lived from a fake, phony, victimized, earthly, sensual, and devilish form of myself. Even when I learned and began to believe that God created me for victory, the disrupters remained in place. Knowing that grace is much more than "unmerited favor" did not mean that I used the grace power to overcome. That's why many of my days, nights, and years remained stagnant.

Until and unless we operate in our Kingdom assignments, the demonically assigned disrupters intended to keep me, you, and everybody else from ever fulfilling God's original intention remain in place. We'll maintain the disrupted agenda: disobedient, stubborn, hardhearted, fearful, zealous for an unrighteous cause, unteachable, rebellious, and stuck.

My life had been spiritually disrupted, and remained so until I began to consistently submit myself step-by-step to the Holy Spirit's guidance. He let me know that it isn't just in intercessory prayer that I am to release spiritual disrupters of the Heavenly kind. The grace to overcome is also the fuel necessary to become the disruption that spiritual assignment against us. When we choose to manifest as sons of God, we demonstrate sonship dominion over darkness.

> And lest I should be exalted above measure by the abundance of the revelations, a thorn in the flesh was given to me, a messenger of Satan to buffet me, lest I be exalted above measure. Concerning this thing I pleaded with the Lord three times that it might depart from me. And He said to me, "My grace is sufficient for you, for My strength is made perfect in weakness." Therefore most gladly I will rather boast in my infirmities, that the power of Christ may rest upon me.
> —2 Corinthians 12:7-9

Look at how Paul had to step up his game to deal with the disrupters assigned to stop him from completing the ministry God had assigned him to fulfill. The satanic spirit sent to beat him down hinder him, whether with a sickness, a pain, or some other kind of physical ailment, was on a mission to disrupt Paul's progress. He says He went to God for help, possibly with one of those, *"Lord, the devil is bothering me, please make him stop,"* kind of pleas. But he was told, *"I've given you the superpower called grace—activate it and watch how it will deal with the thing coming against you."* I know, it's not a properly exegeted paraphrase, nor are we going to do an Aramaic or Greek breakdown right now. Instead, let's use a 21st century lens and look closer at Paul's situation.

"My ministry has been thriving. The Kingdom words I'm releasing are making a change in the lives of Jews and Gentiles. The devil isn't happy and sent a disruption—a personal attack against me. It's supposed to stop me. Admittedly, I thought God handled this kind of stuff, but Jesus let me know that He's given me access to the same weapons He used while walking on Earth.

The Lord let me know that His grace is a superpower from Heaven. It is activated by my humility and trust in Him. I am to stay with my assignment, regardless of how the devil has been making me feel. So, since I'm not about to quit preaching this message of the Kingdom, I'm going to allow God's grace to turn me into a divinely empowered spirit-son disruptor, and unleash Heaven's power to jam the frequencies of this disrupter that's been working me over. Basically, I'm going to let the devil know, *'Your regularly scheduled harassment against me is disrupted by sonship power and the words I'm authorized to release from God's Kingdom.'* That's what I did, and Heaven took care of the rest."

So, what exactly am I saying? The realization that I am a divinely assigned spiritual disrupter, deployed to overcome every weapon formed against me awakened a fight and recognition of purpose within. **I am** graced to take down the disruptions assigned to stop me. **I am** a spirit-son Kingdom disrupter. Wowza! And the funny thing is how right it feels, like, *"Yes, this is me."* I believe that this kind of spiritual recognition contributes to awareness of our true identity. I'm telling you, the inward light just keeps getting brighter. That is one of the cool manifestations I've experienced during the writing of this book.

Lesson to learn: We can preach, teach, and even have a vast reach among people. We can have money, status, and all the other stuff that we might believe are the hallmarks of success in this present era. However, world-class standards are limited to what the kingdoms of this world can produce. Their merchandise does not resonate with God's definition of success. Please understand, we need the Holy Spirit's guidance. Without Him, we cannot and will not access the Kingdom standard that releases dynamic sonship power like Jesus did. It is only through Him that we successfully exercise the authority and deliverance power that sonship provides. We work with Him to remove and destroy the disrupters in our lives.

Let me repeat this realization: Weapons that form against you are meant to be taken out by or through you. It is your honor to manifest this truth: If it can't take out Jesus, the Son of God, then son of God, it also cannot take you out. More than conquerors, remember? Becoming a spiritual disrupter is part of our quest assignment. Now that we know, we can start to gear up for the takedown. Refuse to continue to live from a counterfeit identity. You are a spirit-son of God!

Okay, let's move on to the next lesson to see how it's done.

CHAPTER 15
THE TRUTH ABOUT BROKENNESS

> "What do you mean, 'If I can'?" Jesus asked. "Anything is possible if a person believes." The father instantly cried out, "I do believe, but help me overcome my unbelief!"
>
> — MARK 9:23-24 NLT

In the fifth chapter of Mark's gospel, we saw some of the workings of an unclean spirit in the account of the man in Gadara. Mark actually makes four additional references to unclean spirits, which gives us a very good idea of how focused the demonic is to destroy God's agenda for humanity. I find it interesting that a number of Christians refer to the possibility of being made whole, yet regard wholeness with hope that it will one day be ours. That split mind possibly stems from two causes: our long-term familiarity with brokenness, and a lack of Kingdom spirit-sonship understanding of being made whole.

There are any number of days when you may feel like you are broken. You can describe your emotional, financial, or physical pain; how your body, mind, or emotions are not functioning well, and you just feel totally disconnected from your life or own self. Yet, the truth is that Jesus' sacrifice on Calvary's altar, and the indwelling presence of the Holy Spirit has brought a change for the spirit-sons of God. **We may still think, believe, and act** as though it is so, **but we ourselves are no longer broken**.

To gain the true understanding of wholeness, we must have the heavenly perspective on brokenness. Restoration is intended for us to enjoy as manifested sons of God. Our current rhetoric and beliefs about our born-from-above humanity must conform to Heaven's reality, meaning that we still have areas where we must exchange our worldview of life for the Kingdom view.

It's interesting to look at the healings people experienced in the Gospels—particularly those that tell us that they were *"made whole."* What you see is a spiritual impact that reached beyond the physical recovery into the very souls of the men and women that encountered Jesus. The Greek word, *sōzō* reveals that being made whole is beyond the curing of diseases. In each case, there was a restoration of identity, dignity, and value.

THE TRUTH ABOUT BROKENNESS

To be *made whole* means far more than the absence of sickness; it means reintegration—spirit, soul, and body—into covenant alignment with God's and His Kingdom. When Jesus spoke to the woman cured of the flow of blood, Bartimaeus, being blind no more, or the one leper who returned to give thanks, Jesus did not just acknowledge their faith. They were restored to society, capability, and worth.

While the New Testament speaks of sozo, woven throughout the Old Covenant are stories revealing how God has always been committed to the complete restoration of our lives. Through words like *rapha* (made whole, heal, cure, repair), shalem/šālôm (peace and wholeness), and *tâmîym* (whole, complete, upright), we see that our restoration, soundness, and completion is always God's intention.[1] His covenant terms aren't just poetic; they were and still are manifested in Scripture and through numerous present-day testimonies. Every act of healing, every moment of compassion, every declaration of faith releasing wholeness for someone embodies the heart of the same God that called forth provision, restoration, healing, and the peace that has nothing missing or broken long before Jesus came in the flesh to fulfill that promise.*

WHOLENESS—THE DIVINE EXPRESSION OF GOD'S WILL—IS the Kingdom's remedy for the fractured state of humanity.

---

* See Psalm 103:3, Joel 2:23-25 (KJV); cf. Luke 8:48; Mark 5:21-43.

Brokenness does not define us, yet we can still find it present in areas of our lives, the residual debris of unsettled issues or matters. As sons of God, we should know the price to manifest His wholeness has already been paid, should we choose to pursue its manifestation. However, this comes with choosing intimacy with the Holy Spirit in the manner that is available to spirit-sons. This message is simple. As imitators of Christ, it has been given to us to learn how to master the matters of the flesh in the same manner as He did. One necessary change to attain this kind of power is to allow the Spirit of Truth Himself to annihilate all aspects of false identification within you. We do so by yielding our emotions to the power of Holy Spirit. It's only daunting to consider until we begin to believe that whatever God desires of us is always possible.

> Hope postponed grieves the heart; but when a dream comes true, life is full and sweet. —Proverbs 13:12 (VOICE)

You are not broken, but you may well have some broken pieces that interfere with your quest for wholeness. Maybe you're operating with a repetitive **faith confessions** strategy, one that you've used many times before. You're doing the right kinds of things—you ask for everything you want, the fulfillment of dreams and desires, focusing on everything you believe is necessary to fulfill your calling and election, even declaring God's Kingdom will to be done.

However, from **the religious way** you've gone about your confessions, *you may as well be muttering*

incantations. You've mixed tried-and-true religious practices with buzzwords and methods spoken by popular media ministers, complicating matters to the point that your "prayers" seem to be ineffective. Is it possible that you got the vision or idea from God, then made it yours, instead of finding out from Him how He wants things done? Let's look at this issue as a son of God and get a Kingdom principle perspective.

It is true that as you describe what you want, the creative pathway begins to develop. In the Kingdom of God, there is only one direction for you to go—the way of the King. Father's desires and thoughts become the only desires and thoughts you allow yourself to speak. His words become your actions, and your actions propel you toward the fulfillment of God's dream for your life, including the people, places, and things He adds to the vision. We are meant to actualize or manifest our true Kingdom of God destiny according to God, not social media or our own visionary agenda. But our biggest holdup may be the self-destruction carried within our souls.

Cycles of unforgiveness, anger, bigotry, unhealed emotions, and disobedience all keep us spiraling downward. Maybe it's memories of the judgmental words spoken about you by the haters of your existence that you will not release. Desperation or even bitterness can muck up your progress. You know that you've carried the soul fractures, hits, and bruises into your born-from-above life. That's part of why your quest includes healing, soundness, and wholeness. But maybe you're questing in the wrong direction, which would explain why it

OUR QUEST FOR IDENTITY

feels like you're not getting anywhere. Or you keep trying to put the wrong solutions into place. You could just be recycling the same scenes in your mind and your actions. Continually going around the mountain. Let me give you an example.

AT THE TIME I BEGAN WRITING THIS CHAPTER, MY birthday was a few weeks away. The mental assault began as the day drew nearer, when I began to experience a series of thoughts designed to bring me into a place of depression, possibly with the intent to get me to entertain suicidal thoughts. I experienced feelings of sadness, despair, failure, rejection, and a sense of uselessness for even being in this world—just a bunch of emotional uglies. The thoughts that slammed against my mind were vicious, all focused on what seems to be missing from or lacking in my life. I knew they were demonic assaults against my soul, and it felt like I was getting sapped with words.

However, I really am a Kingdom of God citizen, and the mind that comes from above began to respond on my behalf. As I said, the mental assault was vicious *and* brutal. But the one thought hurled at me, the one I believe that was intended to send me into a pit of despair, turned out to be the very words that caused me to reach within my heavenly arsenal and take it down. I love the words that were written by the prophet Isaiah: *"But in that coming day no weapon turned against you will succeed. You will silence every voice raised up to accuse*

THE TRUTH ABOUT BROKENNESS

you. These benefits are enjoyed by the servants of the LORD; their vindication will come from me. I, the LORD, have spoken!"* The words meant to send me into a downward spiral were, *"All of these years and you're still fat."*

Excuse me? No I'm not. Two reasons. One, I'm a spirit, and spirits don't gain weight. Second, my body has not consistently carried excess weight without a change all these years. That was a lie, and I was commissioned [and ready] to release the Truth into the atmosphere of my mind. Over the past ten years, I have successfully eliminated well over 100 pounds of excess flesh off of my body, most recently within the past three years. Yay me! And within those same years, I have tragically added a great many of those pounds right back. Over and over again, a pattern of advancement and lost ground has played out in my life. It was what some refer to as *a vicious cycle.* In fact, staying at my divinely designed size was a victory that I could not seem to maintain. That's when I received this insightful nugget:

When I ask the wrong questions, I will not receive the right answer.

Meaning, my frustration over my seeming failure kept my focus on, "How do I get the weight off? Again?" And that's when the Holy Spirit prompted me to ask the right question: ***"Why do I keep regaining it?"*** So, I asked the Lord,

---

* Isaiah 54:17, NLT.

"Why do I keep regaining the weight?" It seems that's what He had been waiting for me to say. And oh my, did He ever begin to answer!

In the following chapters, we'll discuss additional portions of what He uncovered. It's going to get really ugly, so if you're looking for a sweet revelation and a quick breakthrough, it will not be found here.

CHAPTER 16
CAN YOU HANDLE THE TRUTH?

For we wrestle not against flesh and blood, but against principalities, against powers, against the rulers of the darkness of this world, against spiritual wickedness in high places. Wherefore take unto you the whole armour of God, that ye may be able to withstand in the evil day, and having done all, to stand.

— EPHESIANS 6:12-13

Evil spirits are predators. Once they have access to someone's mind, will, and emotions, they fight to maintain their feeding ground. They feast on humanity's pain, perpetual sadness, depression, and traumatic memories — those are their troughs. Pride-influencing spirits seek to entice their prey to wear a mask of pretense—a brittle facade that is really a death mask, one that causes individuals to outwardly insist that they are happy, whole, and free—all things they actually are not. Meanwhile there is an inward disintegration of the hopes, dreams, and vision that God intended them to live out.

So, what's really going on? Well, we don't always recognize our true adversary. Our flesh has become so familiar with his ways that we have taken them as our own. Thus we fail in small instances to learn who to stand for and what to destroy. I'll share this little nugget gleaned from the Holy Spirit: ***"It may seem or feel familiar, but it's not me."* Stop identifying with evil. It's not who you are!**

> "...No weapon formed against you shall prosper, And every tongue *which* rises against you in judgment You shall condemn. This *is* the heritage of the servants of the LORD, And their righteousness is from Me," Says the Lord. —Isaiah 54:17

DURING THE TIME OF THIS PARTICULAR MESSAGE, THE prophet Isaiah had a word from God for the exiled people of the nation of Israel. God wanted them to know that regardless of all that was against them, He Himself is greater than any weapons their enemy used. Regardless of the words that they hurled at them, God said that they would be restored. They would be fruitful again. They would overcome. God had assigned them to victory, and made Himself the guarantee. This is why Jesus never lost an encounter with evil. He overcame every demonic attempt against Him with the power of the Kingdom of God. He was set like flint in the belief that there was no possibility of failure, because His assignment in the earth was to restore the Kingdom to us.

Do you know why the weapons formed and fashioned to work against you for destruction **are not supposed to triumph** against you? It's because the **grace to overcome** is part of our Kingdom sonship identity. We are commanded to overcome evil with good. The demonic realm assigns familiar works of evil words, emotions, thoughts, or circumstances against us to keep us in mediocrity and confusion. But *our true identity in the Kingdom includes an assignment against that which is assigned to take us out.* The truth is, we were created, deployed, then assigned to overcome every obstacle that comes against our mission.*

For over twenty-eight years, I remained unaware of the hostile takeover of my life. Sorrow and grief clouded my thinking, influenced by childhood traumas and unresolved issues. This led to emotional isolation and a self-deceiving lifestyle of cyclical self-abuse. These counterproductive actions contradicted my natural way of living. I can attest to the tortuous mind stressors and distorted vision that comes with a victimized perspective. In my case, I chased wrong

---

* See Luke 10:19, John 16:33, Romans 12:21, 1 John 2:13-14, 1 John 4:4-6, 1 John 5:4.

relationships in hopes of disproving my internal malfunctions. I was desperate not to look messed up, so I chased after imaginary relationships that messed me up. Something wrong was at work inside me, determined to destroy my life.

In Ephesians 6:14-18, Paul goes on to speak of the spiritual covering that enables us to stand: truth-girded loins, righteousness as a breastplate, and a readiness to stand on our feet. God's peace has prepared us to stand, regardless of the opposition. He tells us that we have God's faith as our shield, and His word is our sword. Every fiery thought that darts at our minds can be replaced with a true word. And how do we do it? By the utterance of the Holy Spirit, our source of truth and peace. He speaks Kingdom edicts through us in our legal petitions (prayers). This is an example of how we release royal power while living from the right mind.

Learn to recognize where you must actualize true God-given sonship identity. **Hint:** it is always vital to do so in the places where you just want to fit in with everyone else. That surface picture of success that you're coveting is a forgery. Wherever you resist manifesting sonship to maintain the approval of others, you are being led astray. Check closer, and you'll find out that in those instances, love of the Truth is not a part of your arsenal. This means that honesty and transparency are not working from within. Internal weaknesses of character cannot be strengthened with God's might. We do not develop properly, thus we keep speaking and wailing like victims wondering why all of these bad things keep happening to us.

Please understand, **the wrong question will not put you on the path of the right answer.** Instead of asking God "why" questions about circumstantial issues, try asking the Holy Spirit about the broken pieces in your soul and the distorted beliefs at work in your mind, will, and emotions. Believe me, He will answer you—Heaven is fully invested in your deliverance, breakthrough, and manifestation of sonship. Kingdom sonship identity flows from our internal spirit to the outward person. And it takes willingness:

1. First to allow the Spirit of truth to reveal Himself to us,
2. Second to be willing to look at and see what He shows us without making excuses, and
3. Third, accepting Him as our only source for truth so that the will of God can have preeminence within us.

Imagine looking at yourself through a distorted lens, trying to confirm an appearance that isn't yours, hoping to make it true. You're looking at an unhappy person, one that is not free or whole, unable to treat themselves as God wants. That's what I did while trying to fix myself, and the desperation I exuded attracted shady, predatory men, even though they claimed to be Christians.

The ability to see ourselves in God's mirror, the way that He designed and sees us, must be in place **before** we can truly manifest the sonship identity that the Earth and the world is waiting to behold.

CHAPTER 17
BROKEN PIECES & ESTABLISHED PATTERNS

A GLAD HEART MAKES A HAPPY FACE; A BROKEN HEART CRUSHES THE SPIRIT.

— PROVERBS 15:13

"Do I love you?" That is what I asked him the first time he kissed me. He answered, "Yes, you do," to which I replied, "Okay," which is how I was able to enter into marriage with the idea that we would last forever. After all, we were both Christians, faithful church workers, and we talked about mostly everything. We talked about God. We talked about marriage and children. We talked about our past relationships. Sex. Skin tones. Fears. Expectations, etcetera. We talked and we talked and we talked. But I don't think we actually listened to ourselves or one another.

At first he was my friend. But when we became spouses and lovers, the friendship died. Going in, I knew there were things about me that he did not care for; my size and other physical imperfections being the primary issues on the table. In our early talks, we tacitly agreed that I was the flawed one, so I would be the one that changed to become what he wanted me to be. And thus, the course for a marital train wreck was established.

By the end of our first week of marriage I began to experience feelings similar to buyer's remorse. Something felt off, but I attributed it to adjusting to change. My wedding ring felt like an anvil on my finger. Heavy and weighted, so much so, that after a few years I stopped wearing it altogether. Three or four anniversaries passed before I realized that I married a person that did not even like me. We were both emotionally fragmented. It wasn't the different colors of our skin, it was the unresolved issues within our respective souls that brought on the problems... and solidified the emotional abuse patterns.

These small details are given because they factor into the nuggets I'm about to share. However, the point of this chapter is not the imbalance of expectations, verbal abuse or the failed marriage. Therefore, out of respect to the man whose name I once carried, I will talk about my personal failings and omit him as much as possible from the gist of this discussion. He's a good man, we just were not good for one another.

BROKEN PIECES & ESTABLISHED PATTERNS

IN CHRIST, WE OURSELVES ARE NOT BROKEN, BUT THE human experience includes a variety of disappointments, breakdowns and breakaways that leave fragments and particles within our physical and emotional being. Even when we are born-from-above, chances are good we have a trunkful of unsolved mysteries, hurts, and hidden triggers lying dormant in our souls. Which is why, it is the broken pieces of our souls that I want to tell you about.

> **My days are over. My hopes have disappeared. My heart's desires are broken.** — Job 17:11 NLT

As you know, I'm on my own quest while writing this book. What you don't know is how much every paragraph I write costs me, as transparent truth is required. The realization that I have harbored a number of broken pieces within my being has become a powerful incentive to learn how to take hold of my identity. Fragments, shards, splinters—remnants of my shattered, traumatized, violated, and outraged soul—that's what these broken pieces were.

As I shared in the previous chapter, along the way I've learned that **I must ask the correct question to receive the truth I need to change.** I wanted to be made whole, but I had yet to know what wholeness looks like on me, and so my quest was kept in stasis until the Holy Spirit released the necessary intel for breakthrough. I think it would be best to provide you with the facts, then I'll be able to share the encounters of wellness I have experienced.

OUR QUEST FOR IDENTITY

YOU MAY KNOW THAT DIVORCE SIGNIFIES THE DEATH OF A marriage, and that it cuts on all sides. I was married for nine years. I have been divorced for the last 28-plus. I did not become a divorcée, instead I became a wife without a husband... a legal judgement widow. My spouse was not deceased, it was my marriage that died, but I had to go on living—and I subconsciously did so in the same pattern as the marriage. The time I could have spent mourning this marital death was spent establishing a survival-mode mindset. I had to learn how to become a working mother, then how to maintain a single-parent household.

I never consciously mourned the death of my marriage, so the emotional pain that I should have acknowledged and dealt with became burrowed deep inside various places within my soul. Grief found places to hide and abide in the subconscious and unconscious areas of my mind, emotions, thoughts, and beliefs. Emotionally, I still identified with the man of Gadara. Can you see the graveyard and tomb parallel?

It was difficult to keep us housed properly, and I was not always able to do so. There was rent, utilities, after school childcare, clothing, groceries, various jobs, inconsistent income, custody issues, transportation, and the emotional needs and wants that come with raising a preschool-aged child. There was no good time to be sick, medical insurance was occasional depending upon my employment status. I had no time to feel, I was supposed to be strong and courageous, and in part due to past trauma, I no longer knew how to express my emotions or cry.

Trust me, I did not have my act together, nor was I a good manager of money, time, resources, or myself. It was a horrible struggle, and while I had strong family support, there were a few people that watched me from a distance, waiting for my epic fails—which I had, over and over again. Strange as it may seem, I did not know how to ask for the help that I really needed. That false, prideful *"I can handle it"* mindset can be a wicked weapon of self-destruction.

I should mention that I was not morbidly obese when I married. If anything, I was about twenty pounds or so from ***my*** ideal of the perfect size. The subconscious weight gain occurred over the years as we played out various scenes of marital trauma drama. So, what does this story have to do with broken pieces? Quite a bit actually, it is part of the revelation the Holy Spirit released to me in response to my query of ***why*** I kept gaining the weight back.

His answer to my question came in the early morning hours—first as a nugget of truth. Then came His instruction in the ways of wisdom, knowledge, and understanding. I'd worn a shroud of widowhood for almost thirty years. Part of the weight I held on to was like a security blanket, the grief of a woman in mourning. Let's go to the Scriptures for a better explanation.

A BEREAVED PERSON TYPICALLY EXPERIENCES SADNESS, sorrow, and grief over the death of loved ones. **Grief**, according to *Webster's 1828 Dictionary* is partially defined as, "*the pain of mind produced by loss, misfortune, injury or evils of any kind; sorrow; regret.*" **The pain of mind?** Those words caught my attention to the point that I had to know more.

Did you know that you will not find the term, *spirit of grief* in the Bible, but you will find its description within scriptures that talk about sorrow? Consider what King Solomon had to say, *A merry heart taketh a cheerful countenance: but by sorrow of the heart the spirit is broken.* Solomon then presents an interesting contrast to his own words: *Sorrow is better than laughter: for by the sadness of the countenance the heart is made better.**

Sorrow of the heart is another interesting expression. It speaks of honesty within the emotions. A happy heart produces a happy face, whereas a heart of sorrow, if not addressed, can break the connection with our spiritual awareness. But if we pretend to be happy (mask our face) while bearing a sorrowful heart (a heart filled with sadness, a mind filled with pain), we have turned our faces away from the truth covered within. When Truth gets shut off, emotions get suppressed.

This is a form of trauma, where we are not led by the Spirit of

---

* See Proverbs 15:13 and Ecclesiastes 7:3.

God, but by earthly, sensual, and devilish belief systems. Emotional and mental pain patterns subject us to flesh-oriented actions. In other words, your flesh obeys soulish leadings, based on your feelings and physical realm vision. So when we remain in busy or survival mode without a break, we can get distracted by constant urgency, traumatic pain or fear, dulling our spiritual sensitivity. Internal signals—those subtle alerts that something in our emotional or physical life needs attention, can be overlooked. And that's when we ignore symptoms and warnings, pushing aside our feelings to wait for a "better" moment to "deal with matters." Unfortunately, that moment is seldom recognized.

This distraction isn't random. It happens because we've gotten used to wearing masks designed to keep our spirit identity hidden, allowing the counterfeit soul life that is rooted [again, I say] in the earthly, sensual, devilish systems to dominate our self-expression. These masks also keep us "safe" from living out any perspective that clashes with our feelings. We don't hear truth, because the pain is muted—what we call manageable—obscuring our ability to hear our spiritual voice.

Over time, the mask becomes so confining, it prevents us from recognizing (seeing or speaking to) our own emotional crises. Instead we harbor untended, festering wounds. This can also be why some people will fake cry, or laugh in moments when crying could bring relief. The laughter is not real—it lacks the power of joy. Because they are void of merriment—the sound comes from a heart that's learned to protect itself through pretense, hiding true emotions and frustrating their ability to cry for help.

King Solomon said sorrow is better than laughter because honest sorrow invites truth to enter. An honest face allows the Lord to meet us where we are. Sadness of countenance becomes a turning of the face back to the voice of the Holy Spirit, the One who restores. This turning realigns our hearing, softens our hearts, and repositions us to spiritually receive and follow His voice as He leads us out of emotional captivity and into God's definition of wholeness.

Solomon's use of the word we know as *sorrow* is depicted in two Ancient Hebrew translations. The Hebrew word **AhTsB** ('atstsebeth') is used in Proverbs 15:13, meaning to be in emotional pain from grief or heavy toil. It is to grieve, displease, hurt, vex, worship, wrest [think wrestling]. The Hebrew word, **KAhS (ka`as)**, used in Ecclesiastes 7:3 is described with words such as: anger, provoke, grieve, indignation, sorrow, vex, wrath | grief, provocation, sore, spite. These are not just descriptive terms, because each word can also be expressed through actions and reactions fueled by human emotions; things we feel, have felt, are expressing, or have buried within.

Whether we move toward the earthly, sensual, devilish nature of our flesh, or allow the Holy Spirit to lead us, ***we are*** motivated by a spiritual force. I definitely experienced all of them. The prophet Jeremiah spoke of Rachel weeping for her children, but refusing to be comforted, because her children were no more. Conversely, in what is known as the beatitudes, Jesus said that those who mourn are blessed, for they shall be comforted.* So **how** then, can comfort become a blessing?

THE DECISION TO END MY MARRIAGE WAS MINE. Typically, I am not a quitter, so this was a difficult choice to make. I remember crying as I came to the conclusion that it was either divorce, die, or someone would end up in hospital or jail. Calculating the ongoing aspects of the relationship, all I could see was endless years repeating the same distressful scenarios. I did not want to go to jail, end up in hospital, or die. Believing I only had one other option, I chose divorce, but the exit process took over two years. During the marriage, I cried a lot of self-pity and anger tears. But, after I made the decision to end it, I was done with crying, while still in pain.

Then, once the actual divorce decree was executed, I refused comforting, since I pretended that I did not mourn for the marriage that was no more. My heart had become so hard I was trapped in an emotional prison. Unknowingly, I had aligned with a demonic influence assigned to swaddle me in grief that had the appearance of happiness. You see, a sorrow-filled heart will only heal and move toward wholeness from the wounds of traumatic living **when it is submitted to God for comfort.** This means that all of the pain,

---

* See Jeremiah 31:15, Matthew 2:18, and Matthew 5:4.

disappointment, hurt, shame, bitterness, resentment, and residual effects of abuse are to be given to Him.

However, my hardened heart held a myriad of broken pieces—pain, shameful memories, spiteful words, anger, disappointment, frustration, distrust, self-loathing, embarrassment, betrayal, fear and rage—all wrapped in a brittle shroud of torment, pride, covered in pretense. Yes, my very own self-fortified heart refused the comfort of the Holy Spirit. My own soul disallowed wholeness an entry, denying my heart the opportunity of opening to release the toxicity within.

When the Light of Truth broke through my understanding, the first wrappings of that brittle shroud began to shatter inside of my mind, will, and emotions. It felt like a storm of glass shards were blowing and cutting in every direction within me. In one piercing moment of clarity, I began to perceive the diabolical evil that had worked within my own thinking all these years. God's sceptre of righteousness, the right to declare Him Lord even over my legal widowhood, had mercifully been extended toward me.

> Fear not, for you will not be put to shame; And do not feel humiliated, for you will not be disgraced; But you will forget the shame of your youth, And the reproach of your widowhood you will remember no more. —Isaiah 54:4 NAS95

My counterfeit identity declared that I was broken, and I believed this to be true. However, the Holy Spirit taught me that because He abides within me that my perception of brokenness was a lie. He is my wholeness, so how could I be broken? The Holy Spirit supplies Heaven's peace, and that is what He used to replace what I learned were the fragments of broken vows, old grief, and emotional regrets that I had held onto. Then, He made it clear that these broken pieces and soulish debris needed to be discarded. And that's precisely what He began to do. Throw them away. However, the real work had just begun. Imagine my shock when He gave me a posit to consider—a truth so deeply rooted in divine origin that it stands immovable, even when unseen by the human eye.

POSITS GOVERN POSSIBILITIES, AND HE GAVE ME A systemic shockwave when these words formed a question within me:

What If I Chose To Live Life
As Though I Had Never Been Touched?

Notice, the question is not asking me to deny the defilements that happened in the past. The question I needed to consider is if I am willing to see the possibility of living beyond the earthly reality and mental torment of my past, to take on Heaven's perspective of my life? He didn't mean escaping the reality of my body, I'd already done that. I already knew the struggle of the counterfeit identity, He was not recommending pretending these things had never happened. This was mega different. I was being presented an opportunity to see how to live as a spirit-son from the reality of the finished realm. And so, I asked Him the [to me] obvious question. *"What does that look like, Lord?"* As often occurs, my answer was given with a snippet from scripture. This time it came from John 1:46.

> And Nathanael said to him, "Can anything good come out of Nazareth?" Philip said to him, **"Come and see."**[1]

And thus I was given the next step in my quest.

> *Come and see the reality of what is possible on the other side of, "What if..."*

To which I replied, *"Yes, Lord. Let's do that."*

CHAPTER 18
REPENTANCE: THE SUPERPOWER OF SONS

Repent, for the kingdom of Heaven is at hand.

— MATTHEW 4:17

Repentance is one of the most misused superpowers in our Kingdom of God arsenal. That's because it is viewed more as a ritual than the divine extension of the King's scepter. Over the years, I've encountered a number of church people that view repentance as a quick confession of a sinful action, sorrow for wrongdoing, an emotional admission, or even an act of religious penance for bad behavior. Part of our issue might be that repentance is considered to be a doctrinal practice.

But the Greek word for repentance, **Metanoeō**, takes us far beyond a quickly expressed "I repent" apology, or "Oops, busted. Time to repent" kind of behavior. In reality, repentance is a **Kingdom sonship superpower**—a spiritual action and a directive. It calls for a change of mind, behavior, purpose, or intention. As spirit-sons, we get to view repentance as part of our Kingdom of God mandate. When we do, life becomes a lot more interesting.

In the early days of Jesus' ministry, there were two men that preached a message placing "repent" and " kingdom" in the same sentence. The first was John, son of Zechariah the priest and Elizabeth, cousin of Mary. He preached as a voice in the wilderness, preparing the way of the Lord, calling the people to repent in anticipation of the kingdom to come. The second man to preach this message was Jesus of Nazareth, restoring the **reality of Heaven's Kingdom into** the Earth—then demonstrating its power through the signs and wonders that followed—not just by observation, but from what He carried within Himself.

Wherever we have a Kingdom command, there is a spiritual instruction that we need to activate.

> Abide in Me, and I in you. As the branch cannot bear fruit of itself, unless it abides in the vine, neither can you, unless you abide in Me. I am the vine, you *are* the branches. He who abides in Me, and I in him, bears much fruit; for without Me you

REPENTANCE: THE SUPERPOWER OF SONS

> can do nothing. If anyone does not abide in Me, he is cast out as a branch and is withered; and they gather them and throw *them* into the fire, and they are burned. —John 15:5-7

When Jesus had that conversation with His disciples, they were gathered around the table for what would be their last Passover meal together. He had washed their feet after finishing their meal, and had spoken of what was about to happen to Him. Perhaps He was soaking up precious moments with these men that had truly become family. Judas had gone out to take care of his business transaction, and the scene indicates that the rest of them were reclining at the table. John's writings contain truly beautiful language. His transcription of the words that Jesus released conveys a great love for his Master. Yet, what was for them an after dinner conversation, is for us a glimpse into how fluidly the Kingdom decrees, declarations, and commands can flow into a conversation.

> Nevertheless I tell you the truth. It is to your advantage that I go away: for if I do not go away, the Helper will not come to you; but if I depart, I will send Him to you. And when He has come, He will convict the world of sin, and of righteousness, and of judgment: of sin, because they do not believe in Me; of righteousness, because I go to My Father and you see Me no more; of judgment, because the ruler of this world is judged.
> —John 16:7-11

When Jesus spoke concerning the soon-coming Helper, it was the second indication that we need heavenly assistance to understand how to obey Kingdom protocols. With that being so, how is it possible that so many of us go around repenting all by ourselves, without the specialized assistance we need from the Holy Spirit? It's quite possible that we do so, because things such as: repentance, forgiveness, and sometimes even prayer have been viewed as soulish actions instead of a Kingdom entrance and occupation within our inner man. In case I missed a few people, let me say it like this: some of us regard repentance as an act or simple prayer, but there are no corresponding actions that reflect an inward change. In order to manifest true repentance in the manner of the Kingdom, we must do so as spirit sons, not as church members. This is what I mean.

IT WAS JUST A SHORT TIME AGO THAT THE HOLY SPIRIT began to talk to me about true repentance. It was an early morning encounter, as many of my conversations with Him seem to begin. Before I go to sleep at night, I tend to pray in tongues, and have dialogue with Him about areas within my heart and actions that are out of alignment. Some of it is expressed frustration, because I "feel" as though I fell short of pleasing Him in my day. And often that is true. Because I really do want to please Him, I bring these issues to Him so that I can change. I've chosen obedience, but have screwed it up on more than one occasion. And it was on one such morning that He spoke to my spirit. I don't want to refine the original statement He made, so I'll keep this raw.

He let me know that the reason I kept experiencing failure in certain areas is that I have not committed. He told me, *"You haven't truly repented."* Wow. That stung. A lot. But I chose to step forward, not backward. So I listened as He gave me the scenario. I saw that my thought process was aimed in the wrong direction—changing the outside me to fix the inside. To better explain, let's go on a bunny trail for a moment. I promise to kill the rabbit so we can get back on track.

Have you ever used body lotion or oil on your skin? We may use it to counteract dryness, or ash (if you know, you know), have smoother skin, or because we want to enhance our personal scent. Whatever the reason, the objective is to enhance our outward appearance. This is how many of us try to apply spiritual truth. Intellectually, it's possible to understand that true change flows from the inside (spirit and soul) to the outside, but we still try to fix the outside to change the inside. In the Kingdom of God, there is no "fake it 'til you make it." As imitators of Christ, fakery is illegal. And bam! I just killed the rabbit. Let's get back to the encounter.

I was trying to repent from the outside. Unbelievable. I have chosen to live an obedient life, but there I was, back to behavior modification, my old nemesis from my early new Christian days. The Spirit of God let me know that it was **how I thought** about myself and my behavior that caused this issue in me. I was doing some serious tweaking [not twerking, mind you], messing up my own mind. Tweaking isn't good for addicts, and it isn't good for one committed to obeying the Word of the Lord. Why? Both types involve a "fix" of some kind.

Divine mercy responded to my cry for help, I learned that I was still operating from a familiar earthly, sensual, devilish spirit mind flow—where I merely agreed with God that a change of mind calls for a change of actions, permanently. Yet, in my natural man brilliance, I failed to see the light. Oh yes, I obeyed the Bible. I was quick to say that I repented. And I had, many times, but *my spirit mind had not changed sides*. My actions (other than when I was trying to be good) were hit or miss at best, because *I had not taken on His mind*. I still wanted to be the spirit in control. Yes, I was just as foolish as Paul describes in Galatians 3:3. This change began in the Spirit, but I wanted to control it in my flesh.

> Let this mind be in you which was also in Christ Jesus… Therefore let us, as many as are mature, have this mind; and if in anything you think otherwise, God will reveal even this to you. —Philippians 2:5; 3:15

And that is what repentance really is. It is a Spirit-to-spirit matter. Exchanging the mind of the counterfeit man for the mind of Christ. I'm a spirit son of God, living as a daughter on the earth. And there I was, still trying to change my mind on my own terms. Only the Holy Spirit can lead us to Kingdom of God-class transformation. Why? Because our Helper, the Governor and royal Change Agent, is *the Holy Spirit*. The call to repent is a Kingdom command that can only be manifested through sonship.

How do I know when true repentance is operating in my life? It is when the evidence is seen. To change my mind is to change my ways AND the way I think about the habits of old. If no change is evident, it is because my motivation is not sourced to the Kingdom of God. I have performed a hypocritical action, modifying my behavior and words to attain an outward appearance, while my heart, mind, and desires are still connected to the deadness of my flesh. The principle of what Jesus spoke to the scribes and Pharisees is obvious, as they refused to truly repent.

> Woe to you, scribes and Pharisees, hypocrites! For you cleanse the outside of the cup and dish, but inside they are full of extortion and self-indulgence. Blind Pharisee, first cleanse the inside of the cup and dish, that the outside of them may be clean also. Woe to you, scribes and Pharisees, hypocrites! For you are like whitewashed tombs which indeed appear beautiful outwardly, but inside are full of dead men's bones and all uncleanness. —Matthew 23:25-27

True repentance is not just about leaving behind sin—it is about manifesting as a new creation. It is about returning to the Father, stepping into sonship, and accessing the power of the Kingdom. Without it, instead of transforming into mature sons, believers remain pretenders, trapped in cycles of guilt.

> When the Day of Pentecost had fully come, they were all with

one accord in one place. And suddenly there came a sound from heaven, as of a rushing mighty wind, and it filled the whole house where they were sitting. Then there appeared to them divided tongues, as of fire, and *one* sat upon each of them. And they were all filled with the Holy Spirit and began to speak with other tongues, as the Spirit gave them utterance. —Acts 2:1-4

The scripture in Acts tells us that the Helper we need to bring about the change required to walk in true anointing and power has come. The Holy Spirit Himself is the fire needed for our purification of mind, and the languages that He has given to us are key to the process. In his second letter to the church at Corinth, Paul talks to the people about the changes they have made since he rebuked and brought correction. They were very extreme in their ability to be liberal and tolerant of the actions of others, even unto sexual sins and the like. He is glad that they have heeded his correction, but now needs them to pull back from being too extreme in the opposite direction.

Now I rejoice, not that you were made sorry, but that your sorrow led to repentance. For you were made sorry in a godly manner, that you might suffer loss from us in nothing. For godly sorrow produces repentance *leading* to salvation, not to be regretted; but the sorrow of the world produces death. For observe this very thing, that you sorrowed in a godly manner: What diligence it produced in you, *what* clearing *of yourselves, what* indignation, *what* fear, *what* vehement desire, *what* zeal,

REPENTANCE: THE SUPERPOWER OF SONS

what vindication! In all *things* you proved yourselves to be clear in this matter. —2 Corinthians 7:9-11

Godly sorrow brings about repentance, and there is fruit to be seen. Paul speaks of their diligence, and **clearing of self**, indignation, fear of the Lord, and a sense of vengeance (vehement desire); all that they went through to rid their church of the stain upon them. Now, that was to a church about a specific situation, and he talks about how they not only dealt with the sin, but they dealt with themselves. This is when we begin to see the possibilities that repentance gives us. Let's add up what we know about repentance based on the scriptures we've read. It is:

- A change of mind.
- A change of actions.
- A change of perspective.
- A change of kingdoms.
- A change of heart.
- A commitment to get rid of all opposing beliefs and practices.
- A royal commandment to be obeyed.
- A spiritual encounter required of Kingdom sons.
- A spiritual judgment of darkness.
- A Holy Spirit activated superpower, released to bring spiritual sons into the reality of the mind of Christ at work with us.

I'm going to repeat this statement: **True repentance is a superpower** given to us from God to bring us into the sonship transformation process. This is about turning into the something—the someone—that God intends for us to be. So if we see it as an entrance into Kingdom sonship, unlocking power that only belongs to those who have been transformed, we must begin to view repentance as a Kingdom key, not just a decision we make on our own. We are called into a supernatural moment of recognition, a Holy Spirit encounter where everything we once thought was reality is shattered, and Kingdom truth is revealed. Without this encounter, repentance remains shallow, something tried in human strength rather than empowered by the Spirit. When Peter preached in Acts 2:38, saying, *"Repent, and be baptized... and you will receive the gift of the Holy Spirit,"* he wasn't calling people to feel sorry that they had sinned. He was calling them into a new reality—one where repentance is the doorway to transformation, the Spirit is the means of empowerment, and sonship is the result.[1]

Consider true repentance from a sonship perspective—is it of the flesh, soul, or the spirit? The answer is spirit, affecting the soul, correcting the flesh. Because when true change begins to come forth, it comes from deep within our being. This is why we are not just talking about turning from sin. Repentance is a denouncement of the false images of ourselves, the one filled with sins, transgressions and iniquities from the anti-Kingdom life. When we truly repent, we have chosen to be rid of all things that pertain to the earthly, sensuous, and

REPENTANCE: THE SUPERPOWER OF SONS

devilish imagination used to build a false image of ourselves—one that we worshipped on a foreign altar.

Now, by looking at God's intention in calling us to repentance, the possibility of a permanent life transformation alters our old traditional perception. By viewing repentance as a spiritual encounter with Heaven instead of a few mumbled words after every mistake—we realign with God's original intent—sonship identity. We develop an abhorrence, disgust, and a turning away from doing or being anything that is grievous to the Holy Spirit. We want nothing to do with those old things ever again. Think of it as a final breakup. **"Take all of your nasty stuff with you. Get out! Never, ever come back. I sever all ties with you. Don't even think about calling me again. Delete my phone number. I don't want my name to even be associated with you. Take it off your tongue! I banish you and everything to do with you from my heart, mind, thoughts, memories, and life, for all eternity!"**

Too much? Not really. When you truly repent, everything that is truly you declares, *"I want no part of that thought, action, activity, or life ever again. Never again will I think, act, or entertain any ideas of doing, saying, thinking, or being connected with the works and ways of the devil."* In the Name of Jesus, declare it to be so! Without this shift in our thinking, true repentance does not manifest. Now our question is, how do we get to this point, spiritually?

Repentance is an essential portal that we must enter into by way of the Sonship Door, our Lord Jesus Christ. Because it takes the Light of the Son to manifest the Kingdom of God on earth—through obedient sons.

Now we come to the big question.

Have you truly repented the way the King of kings commanded?

Or are you still trying to change your mind and life on your own terms?

This is a question that only the Spirit of Truth can answer for you.

So, *Ask Him*.

CHAPTER 19
A SECOND REPENTANCE SPIRITUAL ENCOUNTER

Something happened the day after I wrote the previous chapter. I was stirred in my spirit that it was time to apply what I had learned about the true repentance principle. Throughout the day, questions rolled around within my spirit mind. These were topics that I planned to speak with the Holy Spirit about when I went to bed. And that night, I talked to Him specifically about what I wanted most to know: **How do I enter the realm of repentance through Jesus?**

And the Lord Jesus Himself answered me. I got to talk to both of them. I'm tearing up a bit as I type this, because my God is so real! The Lord told me that He heard my call. He said that I didn't have to "do" anything except take His hand. No, I didn't have a vision of Jesus, I saw Him from within. And He was smiling as His hand extended toward me. I came to understand that this was more of a prophetic action that I made than a vision I simply saw. When I reached out to take

His hand, I handed over my mind to Him, giving up ownership of the way that I think, believe, and act. It's like the vocabulary of my mind instantly changed. I kid you not. I can review my actions and see where my path diverges according to which thoughts I follow. I am used to hearing scriptures within as I go about my day, but now, as I hear His words inside of me, the experience is nuanced with a different strength, so much so that I had to join in praise singing hymns of old.

—*from Charles Wesley and Robert Lowry (public domain)*

O, for a thousand tongues to sing
My great Redeemer's praise,
The glories of my God and King,
The triumphs of His grace!
My gracious Master and my God,
Assist me to proclaim,
To spread thro' all the earth abroad,
The honors of Thy name.
Jesus! the name that charms our fears,
That bids our sorrows cease,
'Tis music in the sinner's ears,
'Tis life and health and peace.
He breaks the power of reigning sin,
He sets the prisoner free;
His blood can make the foulest clean;
His blood availed for me.
To God all glory, praise, and love

A SECOND REPENTANCE SPIRITUAL ENCOUNTER

> Be now and ever given
> By saints below and saints above,
> The Church in earth and heaven.

*Oh precious is the flow, that makes me white as snow.
No other fount I know, nothing but the Blood of Jesus.*[1]

When I acted upon the expression of my spiritual sonship desire to truly repent (metanoie), the Door opened Himself to me. And while I trust Him to lead me, it is my honor and responsibility to follow. I do not belong to myself, I belong to Him, my Savior and Owner. I believe that I will live to fulfill my Kingdom destiny. I'm certainly going to walk the talk, but I refuse to make assumptions that could lead to complacency. It's wiser to walk in the Spirit of the Fear of the Lord.

Here's the lesson: It's not our job to perfect ourselves, it is our honor to obey God. My mom preaches that all the time. It took me a while to receive it with God's understanding since, like King Saul, I defined obedience on my own terms. Now, I continually tell myself how much I love to obey God as He defines obedience. You may very well have to do the same thing. It's called renewing your mind.[2]

My talk with Jesus and the Holy Spirit continued through the person of my brother, Apostle Raymond Williams. He and his beautiful wife, Pastor Carrie, are the overseers of *Forbidden To Fail* in Tampa, Florida. As he and I were visiting on Zoom a few days or so later, I shared various parts of my [chapter 17] broken pieces experience with him. He asked me a question—*How whole did I think I was?* I said about 85% or so. He shared a modern day parable based upon the life of someone he knew, then asked, *"What if you never attain 100%?"*

I thought about it, and a realization hit. **It doesn't matter.** That's what I told my brother. Wholeness is our portion, but the way we measure it is the way we reap its benefits. I have an opinion about my life and my person, but God has the vision and original plan. I can either focus on my idea of what's not right or still needs to be fixed within me, or allow the righteousness of God to be the wholeness that brings me to maturity. And that's exactly what happened. In that moment, I recognized that **the Lord Jesus Himself is my manifested wholeness.** He is enough.

So, thank you, my precious brother Raymond—Apostle and truly cool man of God. And thanks to you, my sister Carrie, fabulous, fierce, and faithful, I love you both!

CHAPTER 20
SONSHIP MUST BE MANIFESTED

> BEHOLD, TO OBEY IS BETTER THAN SACRIFICE...
> —1 Samuel 15:22

My greatest struggle to understand the power of my sonship has revolved around food. When it came to my weight, I did not seek the power of grace to help me shed the snakeskin of witchcraft, rebellion, and willfulness in my soul. Mercy has truly kept me, praise God, as I have struggled with breaking through in this one area for over 30 years. What has kept me locked up for so long? Two things: First, ignorance of the difference between that which is familiar and that which is Truth, and second, I nursed a dishonorable attitude toward the Spirit of God.

I walked an interesting path, forged with double-minded choices. Some leaned toward righteousness, others bowed to self-destruction. Outwardly, I imaged compliance, inwardly I was too scared to even spit. Fear was constant, increasing the torment within me. I knew I was still in disobedience, but I didn't know what to do to get into alignment. I had changed my question, and received what turned out to be **the first part** of the answer. The second part occurred during another Holy Spirit encounter, after I had been crying out to Him for help. I was in true fear that I would die as a failure—never completing my Kingdom assignment.

While reading the account of King Saul in 1 Samuel 15, I realized that I was in another level of rebellion. If you don't recall the story, this is the convergence of events that led to the end of his kingship, his days of demonic torment, and ultimately his death. Like Saul, my own heart was filled with a darkened refusal to do the will of God the way He said to do it. I was constantly doing *what I wanted Him to mean*, muting my ears from hearing the truth. I had put my own life in danger.

> **Quick bunny trail detour:** Stories are told about people that have pet snakes. *Why??* Apparently many feel their precious pets are so harmless that they sleep with them. Again, *why??* Well, after a while they notice that their pets don't eat, but they're growing. Long story short — veterinarians have to let the owners know that the reason their slithery bed partners (*WHY????*) are growing but don't have much of an appetite is because they are, you guessed it, preparing to eat their two-legged bed partners. Isn't that just like a snake? And Bam! Let's get back to our lesson.

Well, my issue was the same. In the story, Saul tells Samuel that the judgement of rebellion and disobedience against him was wrong. In the eyes of Saul, he obeyed God to the letter. In the eyes of God and to the ears of Samuel, he had not. And wow! I saw myself in that story. God told me to eat a certain way. I obeyed until I got tired of eating the same things. I was resentful and defiant, which is really stupid. He did not create me to be outwardly beautiful with an ugly-acting soul. And that's precisely how I was acting.

I was winning physically, but God had given me three instructions to follow on the journey. I failed to do one. I changed the plan to fit my convenience, thus **I tried to be the controlling spirit.** Modified obedience is disobedience. Right? As of this writing, I've made progress, and I am on the right path, but **completion once and for all must happen or I fail**. There's no point in my playing games and pretending that I have my act together, because I don't. In fact, I'm not writing this book from perfection. There are raw flaws all over the place.

This journey has brought me to the place where I can honestly say that I do have a different heart and mind. But again, that's not enough. I'm a son of God, a living spirit in the physical body of a beautiful woman. I must manifest His Kingdom excellence and allow the inward beauty of His holiness to radiate through me. Male or female, that's your sonship story too. Weight may not be your issue. It doesn't matter, because regardless of the area where you struggle, you have been given instructions that you must complete. Talk is talk, but sonship obedience **is seen**.

So, here I am, exposing not just a determination to breakthrough, but an intercessor's cry for you as well. My prayer is that you stop claiming to be an obedient son while you behave like an entitled orphan. Or a bastard. Both are outside of the Kingdom of God, because they despise His correction. The true sons of God always take His correction, endure hardship, and **make the change!** We must set our faces like flint, submitting to the power of God that helps us to keep moving forward.*

I know these words bring conviction. Yes, Overcomer, I'm speaking directly to you. You are paying attention. Thank you so much, I'm rooting for all of us. Some have already thrown this book to the side. There are others that read, but will just shake their heads, and find what I say to be completely non-applicable or unrelatable because they don't have my particular set of issues. To be truthful, I don't have the issues either. It's a decision to obey or rebel. That's it.

Finally, once and for all, I've chosen God's definition of obedience. Did you know that when we choose His obedience, we also choose true sonship? That's when the lessons we receive are all about how to live on Earth from Heaven, the place of our citizenship from which we manifest royal victory. We'll get to that in the last few chapters.

---

* 2 Timothy 2:1-6, 4:3-5; Hebrews 12:3-13, Luke 9:51, Isaiah 50:7. The Holy Spirit really does help us when we choose to obey.

SONSHIP MUST BE MANIFESTED

1 SAMUEL 15

"Samuel also said to Saul, "The LORD sent me to anoint you king over His people, over Israel. Now therefore, heed the voice of the words of the LORD. Thus says the LORD of hosts: 'I will punish Amalek *for* what he did to Israel, how he ambushed him on the way when he came up from Egypt. Now go and attack Amalek, and utterly destroy all that they have, and do not spare them. But kill both man and woman, infant and nursing child, ox and sheep, camel and donkey.' So Saul gathered the people together and numbered them in Telaim, two hundred thousand foot soldiers and ten thousand men of Judah. And Saul came to a city of Amalek, and lay in wait in the valley. Then Saul said to the Kenites, "Go, depart, get down from among the Amalekites, lest I destroy you with them. For you showed kindness to all the children of Israel when they came up out of Egypt." So the Kenites departed from among the Amalekites. And Saul attacked the Amalekites, from Havilah all the way to Shur, which is east of Egypt.

He also took Agag king of the Amalekites alive, and utterly destroyed all the people with the edge of the sword. But Saul and the people spared Agag and the best of the sheep, the oxen, the fatlings, the lambs, and all *that was* good, and were unwilling to utterly destroy them. But everything despised and worthless, that they utterly destroyed. Now the word of the LORD came to

Samuel, saying, "I greatly regret that I have set up Saul *as* king, for he has turned back from following Me, and has not performed My commandments." And it grieved Samuel, and he cried out to the LORD all night. So when Samuel rose early in the morning to meet Saul, it was told Samuel, saying, "Saul went to Carmel, and indeed, he set up a monument for himself; and he has gone on around, passed by, and gone down to Gilgal." Then Samuel went to Saul, and **Saul said to him, "Blessed *are* you of the LORD! I have performed the commandment of the LORD."** But Samuel said, "What then *is* this bleating of the sheep in my ears, and the lowing of the oxen which I hear?" And Saul said, "They have brought them from the Amalekites; for the people spared the best of the sheep and the oxen, to sacrifice to the LORD your God; and the rest we have utterly destroyed."

Then Samuel said to Saul, "Be quiet! And I will tell you what the LORD said to me last night." And he said to him, "Speak on." So Samuel said, "When you *were* little in your own eyes, *were* you not head of the tribes of Israel? And did not the LORD anoint you king over Israel? Now the LORD sent you on a mission, and said, 'Go, and utterly destroy the sinners, the Amalekites, and fight against them until they are consumed.' Why then did you not obey the voice of the LORD? Why did you swoop down on the spoil, and do evil in the sight of the LORD?" And **Saul said to Samuel, "But I have obeyed the voice of the LORD, and gone on the**

SONSHIP MUST BE MANIFESTED

mission on which the LORD sent me, and brought back Agag king of Amalek; I have utterly destroyed the Amalekites. But **the people took of the plunder, sheep and oxen, the best of the things which should have been utterly destroyed,** to sacrifice to the LORD your God in Gilgal." So Samuel said: "Has the LORD *as great* delight in burnt offerings and sacrifices, As in obeying the voice of the LORD? Behold, to obey is better than sacrifice, *And* to heed than the fat of rams. For rebellion *is as* the sin of witchcraft, And stubbornness *is as* iniquity and idolatry. Because you have rejected the word of the LORD, He also has rejected you from *being* king."

Then Saul said to Samuel, "I have sinned, for I have transgressed the commandment of the LORD and your words, because I feared the people and obeyed their voice. Now therefore, please pardon my sin, and return with me, that I may worship the LORD." But Samuel said to Saul, "I will not return with you, for you have rejected the word of the LORD, and the LORD has rejected you from being king over Israel." And as Samuel turned around to go away, *Saul* seized the edge of his robe, and it tore. So Samuel said to him, "The LORD has torn the kingdom of Israel from you today, and has given it to a neighbor of yours, *who is* better than you. And also the Strength of Israel will not lie nor relent. For He *is* not a man, that He should relent." **Then he said, "I have sinned;** *yet* **honor me now, please, before the elders of my people and before**

Israel, and return with me, that I may worship the LORD your God." So Samuel turned back after Saul, and Saul worshiped the LORD. Then Samuel said, "Bring Agag king of the Amalekites here to me." So Agag came to him cautiously. And Agag said, "Surely the bitterness of death is past." But Samuel said, "As your sword has made women childless, so shall your mother be childless among women." And Samuel hacked Agag in pieces before the LORD in Gilgal. Then Samuel went to Ramah, and Saul went up to his house at Gibeah of Saul. And Samuel went no more to see Saul until the day of his death. Nevertheless Samuel mourned for Saul, and the LORD regretted that He had made Saul king over Israel." **[Bold emphasis mine]**

I pray that you ask the Holy Spirit to vet you and convict where necessary. If you're frustrated in fulfilling your calling, or still saying that you don't know what it is, you're not reading this by accident. It may be time to ask a different question. Just maybe, you should ask if you are anything like Saul? You do want to know the truth, right?

Now, we've also established that true repentance is a part of our Kingdom sonship reality, and that all of the words spoken concerning our effectiveness in our assignment are sourced from God's divine design for our lives—meaning that we live, move, and have our identity **because** of the words released from Heaven concerning us, meaning **all Kingdom manifestations on Earth are caused by speaking Heaven's words.** I must take you on a quick parallel road trip to solidify the point I'm making.

The weight of our words: It wasn't too long ago that I received a few lessons from the Holy Spirit instructing me on an aspect of intercessory prayer. For the most part, I pray apostolically and prophetically, mantled in the words that have already been released governmentally. That means that a lot of the time, we release disruptions, looking ahead of the current events, to release whatever boundaries or obstructions toward darkness that the Holy Spirit directs us to do. Our prayer team is assigned to speak over certain regions concerning spiritual matters that affect the lives of others. On this particular day, we saw something on the spiritual horizon that needed attention, but sensed that we did not have the utterance necessary to break through. This understanding was intentional on the part of the Holy Spirit. He was letting us know that we had not released enough of Heaven's words to effect the necessary change. The words that we attempted to release in our own understanding had no spiritual weight.

At that point, our frequency level did not release the *"Light Power"* necessary to cut through and make the mark required. But we were far enough ahead of the thing that we could begin to do what was necessary. Here's the point: Heaven's words come into the Earth by way of the spirit words He releases through us. To paraphrase what the Holy Spirit said to me—when you really want to **change matters**, speak in My language. *"...For we do not know what we should pray for as we ought, but the Spirit Himself makes intercession for us with groanings which cannot be uttered. Now He who searches the hearts knows what the mind of the Spirit is, because He makes intercession for the saints according to the will of God. And we know that all things work together for good to those who love God, to those who are the called according to His purpose."**

Well, we began to pray in the Spirit, yielding our tongues to Him for a matter of weeks. We'd pray in the spirit, then release the few English words we had. We did this week after week for about a month or so. Then one day, the words came forth like a torrent, prayed in the language of our understanding. The power of the words was tangible, not because of a cool prayer vocabulary, but because the presence of Holy Spirit Himself was evident as we prayed. The weight of the words was sufficient to change the algorithms of the atmosphere, and to establish the mark of the Kingdom of God in that place. Just like during the Genesis creation days, we needed the voice of the Creator's will

---

* See Romans 8:26-28.

SONSHIP MUST BE MANIFESTED

to be heard by the earth—and just like when Jesus was here, Father again spoke through His sons. Okay, let's get back to the main point.

The LORD owns the earth and all it contains, the world and all who live in it. —Psalm 24:1 NET

WE KNOW FROM THE BOOK OF GENESIS THAT GOD HAS the right to store everything in the Earth necessary to bring forth His heavenly vision—including the provision to fulfill every assignment. The Earth belongs to Him, so what we want to keep in the forefront of our thinking is the reality that Elohim, our Creator God, is the Chief or Father Spirit of spirits. Our first view of Him is as the One that vibrated, brooded, **and spoke** His will into the Earth. This is where it gets really cool. When we consider all that God has done as Creator, and remember that when He spoke in the beginning, creation obeyed. We see that **God's voice is the one that the Earth is conditioned to respond to**. We know that everything that transpired here on Earth happened *because* the Creator of Heaven and Earth released His words into Earth's atmosphere.

Have you ever experienced moments of frustration when you read the word of God, or listen to a minister preach on a topic that fires and inspires you to be different, yet the actual application seems difficult to take hold of? Or how about this: You have a glimpse of what you are here on Earth to do, and you can even see yourself in the location, vocation, or region where the work will get done. Your frustration is that the money you expect, the people you want or need, and everything else keeps getting hindered. Or you can see your physical change—your healing, wholeness, wellness, body sculpting, or whatever kind of breakthrough you know is yours in plain sight—but the struggle to manifest it is wearing you down. I know. I have experienced these moments, especially the frustration, and sometimes, I did not even think about asking the Holy Spirit to give me the question to ask Him.

Remember the parallel road trip we went on? It leads to this question: how much praying in the spirit realm did the Holy Spirit do through you on these issues? If you look back, you've probably spent more time begging or decreeing big things with the frequency power of a wet noodle. Consider this simple probability: because **you have not yet released enough of Heaven's words into the atmosphere**, you also **have not released the Kingdom strategy and sound that brings these things to manifestation.**

To manifest Heaven's kingdom, we do not speak earthly, sensual, and devilish words. Jesus said that His words are spirit and life, *and oh, I'll be glad when I can tell you what I've learned about that.* The spiritual Source and sound of our spirit words must be factored into the whole. What is the spirit origin and quality of your words? Heaven or Earth? Zoe or Sarx?

SONSHIP MUST BE MANIFESTED

Truth. When a Kingdom son looks into the finished realm to see, then speaks what was seen, Earth is authorized to release what Heaven has supplied. Whenever Heaven's words pierce the earthly atmosphere, the Earth responds by yielding to the realities of Heaven. We are spiritual sons. **The words that we speak about our lives must correspond to the Son's image and likeness**. We must speak and sound like Him to bring forth the power that changes this world.

Otherwise, we create monsters.

CHAPTER 21
FAMILIAR PATTERNS, FAMILIAR SPIRITS

I TRULY DELIGHT IN GOD'S COMMANDS, BUT IT'S PRETTY OBVIOUS THAT NOT ALL OF ME JOINS IN THAT DELIGHT. PARTS OF ME COVERTLY REBEL, AND JUST WHEN I LEAST EXPECT IT, THEY TAKE CHARGE.

— ROMANS 7:22-23 MSG

My daughter Arayna and I often interject movie quotes and references into our conversations—we've done it for years. *Galaxy Quest*, a satirical space-age comedy, is one of our go-to movies for fun phrases. It combines elements of the *Star Trek* television franchise with other alien-in-space films. The plot follows the adventures of the former cast of actors from the eponymous television show who, after encountering genuine beings from another planet, assume true hero identities.

In the film, the actors remember the glory days of each season's episodes, their lines, character roles, and the behind the scenes shenanigans. When cast into a real-life drama intertwined with their fictional roles, they somewhat revert back to their characters. **Two of the best quotes from the film:**

1. **In reference to a recurring pattern of averted doom:** *"It always stops at one on the show."*
2. **In response to a failure to perceive a pattern of alien conflict:** *"Did you guys ever watch the show?"*

I mentioned in the previous chapter that at the onset of my marriage, I was roughly twenty pounds from *my* ideal weight. What I didn't tell you is that my ideal weight was **different from** my husband's ideal of what my weight should be. Also, that during the numerous times that I did reverse the excess weight gain, I returned to, but never went below my wedding day weight and size.

I had a "duh" moment, when I began to consider the probability that I have been in an established pattern of familiarity, where I could only go so far, and no further. I'm reminded of the final lyrics in The Eagles' classic, *Hotel California*, sung just before the epic guitar solo. And I wondered:

Did my deep conscious mind create a **check out**? Was I continually living from a counterfeit image of myself—one that looked and sounded like me?

It was like I could **never leave** the recycling defeat.

"It Always Stops At One On The Show." During a spirit language talk with the Holy Spirit, I was shown a key pattern piece submerged in both my subconscious and unconscious mind vaults. It was a subtle self-sabotage, a rebellious instruction to my body: *"This is as low as you go, and no further."* It was an implanted defiance. Since my size was not pleasing to my husband, then I wasn't pleasing to him either. Internally, I rebelled against his requirement that I weigh a specific weight to look a certain way that he deemed acceptable to him. So, according to the patterns of passive defiance, I inwardly determined that **I would go no further down the scale, and if it got too close to acceptable to him, I would go the other way.** That marriage ended years ago, yet over and again, I have played out this tired scene, with no limits on how big my body could get, just how small.

And here's the real kicker—*it always stopped at the same numbers on the scale*. Which is a stupid way to punish someone—especially when you define **stupid** as walking in a familiar cycle of self-sabotage that stemmed from a darkened understanding of my own worth. I was not hurting that man all these years, but I sure have dishonored

God by messing over His temple. Unfortunately, until the time came that I discovered a familiar behavior that was not a true expression of myself, it was my normal.

Moses, when given instructions for the building of the tabernacle and its elements, was admonished to make all things **according to the pattern** he was shown. In the New Testament, Paul told Timothy to **follow the pattern of sound words** that he had received. A pattern is a repetitious picture, design, direction, or outline. Words create pictures and forge pathways. In the earliest days of marriage, my husband and I established an unholy agreement that became the framework for distorted patterns of expectation and behavior, both voiced and internalized.

"Did you guys ever watch the show?" Have you ever had this happen? An action or thought you've performed many times suddenly felt…wrong? It seems familiar, like your body and soul are going through the motions, but your spirit has stepped back and said, "Wait… that's not me." Your "been there or done that," behavior does not bear witness with who you now know that you are in Christ.

The opportunity has been presented to look beyond the usual and see the pattern of events that always cycle back to the same undesired outcome. Those are not déjà vu moments—it is your sonship vision, enabling you to see a crack in the imposter's mask.

> "I ask the glorious Father and God of our Lord Jesus Christ to give you his Spirit. The Spirit will make you wise and let you understand what it means to know God. My prayer is that light will flood your hearts and that you will understand the hope that was given to you when God chose you." —Ephesians 1:17-18a CEV

If you can relate to any of what you're reading, the eyes of your understanding have begun to open. When you can perceive a different version of yourself, the one that diverges from your current behavior, you have reached a point where you are prepared to shed the counterfeit identity and its familiar spirit, which has been imitating you all along. Now, let's move past the pretty words and aha moment.

What was really going on in me? The thing I labeled a subconscious or unconscious implant of defiance —was **the familiar spirit** of my soul—***REBELLION***, the spirit that had tried to make itself one with me. But suddenly, the eyes of my understanding truly lit up, and for the first time, I saw rebellion as more than just a soulish act or hardened heart. I saw it as **an actual familiar spirit**, complete with the **unclean elements** of witchcraft, subtle sorcery, and foul roots of deception. **This familiar spirit** masqueraded as my childhood imaginary friend, and used my childhood trauma and adult pain to form an alliance with me. It was a false comforter that had provided a hooded cloak for me to wear, encouraging me to maintain behaviors that resulted in a lesser version of myself, even while being in Christ. Not possession. Illusion, a false narrative and image. And for years, I had accepted it.

What Is a Familiar Spirit? We'll revisit this deeper in the next phase of our journey, but here's a quick definition. A familiar spirit is a mimicker. A counterfeit. It pretends to be the voice of God—but isn't. It replays your traumas, comforts your dysfunction, enables your self-destructive behavior, and attempts to speak as though it was the Holy Spirit. It isn't. Like the serpent that it is, it twists itself into your emotional logic until you can't tell where it ends and you begin. Unless you use the lens of Truth. For further insight, an online search, concordance, or Bible dictionary provides the Ancient Hebrew pictograph for the word 'Ôb (אוֹב), which is often translated as "medium" or "necromancer."

- **Aleph (א)** – Ox: strength, leader, wineskin
- **Vav (ו)** – Nail: connector, tent peg
- **Bet (ב)** – House or tent

Together it is translated as a wineskin suspended in the tent. An empty vessel, hanging—waiting to be filled. Historically, a familiar spirit worked through an empty "container"—a medium, necromancer, or deceived person whose soul had made room for a false voice.

I have been that container. I really had been operating under the influence of a spirit of divination within my own soul. But that agreement is broken, destroyed. No longer do I say, "Well, that's just how I do things." **No, it is not.** That's how I have reacted to life on earth, but *that is **not** who I am.* The memories, images, feelings and bitter emotions of past pain once echoed louder than the whisper of truth. I was hearing a counterfeit comforter. Not the Spirit of God. Three things I quickly understood:

1. The wicked foolishness bound up in my heart since childhood required Heaven's rod of correction to remove it.
2. This is the reason that my repentance was not true.
3. The witchcraft, disobedience and iniquity of flesh, dared to try and face off with the power of the Spirit of God within me—and failed!

Some reading this can understand the sense of ugliness in the unyielding nakedness of a moment like this. Seeing and being seen. The weeping, revulsion and feeling sick to my stomach, ready to vomit, feeling like something was stuck in my throat, trying to choke me. I felt bowed down with remorse as I released a spate of apologies and weeping. His presence is here, Himself, my beautiful, beautiful Savior, Lord, Redeemer, Warrior, Defender, Brother, and Owner. He is the Lover of my soul. My Deliverer.

Inwardly, I saw myself running out of the tombs, falling at His feet. Worshipping. And He—my Jesus—commanded the familiar to leave me. And it did. Here I am, emptied of those things that have been with me for most of my life. And so I worship. *My Jesus. My Jesus. My Jesus!*

And since this happened to me as I wrote this chapter, I can tell you that I feel a different kind of tired. It's post-battle fatigue, but *I* didn't do the warring. It's so different, like a rest from weariness. I am different. And, I have to tell you, that within me is a knowing I've not had before—it's as though the Holy Spirit has given me leave to say something I have never ever said—not even after my *"I met Jesus under the table in Monterey, California"* encounter.

For the first time in my life, I can say that I am sitting in Jesus' presence, **clothed, and in my right mind.** How is it possible for me to know and share this with you? Because I'm looking through the clean lens of a son of God. I have become His obedient son! **The Son flexed His power again.** This time for me.

My God! My God! My God!

I'm clean!

Thank You. Thank You. Thank You!

Just so you know, I didn't even plan to write this chapter. But oh! I am so glad that I did!

CHAPTER 22
THE POWER OF THE WILDERNESS

> AND JESUS BEING FULL OF THE HOLY GHOST RETURNED FROM JORDAN, AND WAS LED BY THE SPIRIT INTO THE WILDERNESS, BEING FORTY DAYS TEMPTED OF THE DEVIL. AND IN THOSE DAYS HE DID EAT NOTHING: AND WHEN THEY WERE ENDED, HE AFTERWARD HUNGERED.
>
> — LUKE 4:1–2 KJV

Have you ever noticed that when some believers talk about the wilderness, they often describe it as a place of desolation, delay, or even punishment of kind? *"I'm going through a wilderness season,"* typically does not sound like a good time. I find it more than interesting that the Bible tells us that after those forty days, Jesus emerged **in the power of**

the Holy Spirit. And I began to wonder, is it possible that this is the place where His sonship was solidified? Absolutely.

The wilderness has a reputation. It is often seen as a place of chastisement or delay, where destiny is withheld and progress is halted. In our quest, let's take a look at Jesus' *before* and *after* wilderness time through a different lens. We know that God planned it, but why?

What did Jesus witness, hear, and experience that we should know too? If we look through His experience, we will see how the wilderness became His appointed place of divine commissioning. **It was the proving ground of the Son**.

> When all the people were baptized, it came to pass that Jesus also was baptized; and while He prayed, the heaven was opened. And the Holy Spirit descended in bodily form like a dove upon Him, and a voice came from heaven which said, "You are My beloved Son; in You I am well pleased."
> —Luke 3:21-22

Luke recounts **three simultaneous occurrences** that Jesus experienced at His baptism. First, the heaven was opened, next, the Holy Spirit descended upon Him like a dove in **bodily form**, and then, He heard the voice of His Father speak from Heaven, confirming His sonship *and* expressing pleasure in the relationship. **An opening. A descent. A sound.** Wow. Wow. Wow! And then, He received a direction. The Holy Spirit **led Him** into the wilderness. He did not go on His own.

> Then Jesus, being filled with the Holy Spirit, returned from the Jordan and was led by the Spirit into the wilderness, being tempted for forty days by the devil. And in those days He ate nothing, and afterward, when they had ended, He was hungry. —Luke 4:1-2

We read that He was tempted by the devil during these forty days. For many, the chief temptation during any period of fasting is to eat. Thus far, Jesus hadn't done much to be brought on the satan's radar. But many fasts have those moments of regret (I should have eaten more), self-pity (I don't get to eat anything???), exaggerated, dramatic hunger pangs (I'm going to starve. I can't make it!), and even sudden health and nutrition knowledge (I need to eat. This is stupid! Going without a meal isn't good for my body). And let's not forget the mental pictures of all the foods you plan to eat just as soon as this fasting thing is done. You know, the typical disrupters.

However, if you've ever fasted successfully, you know that when your focus shifts away from self, food is the last thing you think about, which, I believe, is precisely what happened with Jesus. What interests me is **what these accounts *do not* say**, which is that during these same forty days, Jesus had the opportunity to spend time getting to know both the Holy Spirit and His Father. Naturally, He would have had momentary hunger twinges, but **the reality of being in the presence of His Father and His Helper would**

satisfy any cravings for food, for surely He was being instructed in the inner workings of the Kingdom of God.

In the wilderness, not only was His Father given full attention, but I believe that Jesus also enjoyed being bathed in the love and comfort of His Father's presence. Not to mention, He had to feel an inward reconnection—the something missing had been found. Would it be too radical to suggest that He found His sonship rhythm? I think He did, because everything about His life now clicked into place—the Godhead was in sync. *A heavenly convergence and royal family reunion* happened in the wilderness: The Father, His Son, and His Spirit of Anointing.

After these meetings, we know that He was tempted after His time of instruction, but never once did the devil triumph. We know he failed, because otherwise, the whole thing would have been over. He tried on three different levels, and these three encounters exposed the purpose of temptation. It was never really about food, it was about power, equality, control, and a desire to rule as a god. To win yet another spirit over to his side—away from how God said things had to be—could be the capstone of all that he sought.

But that did not happen, instead He was rejected, rebuked, and given Heaven's constitutional words with royal power and authority. So the satan left Him, and after that victory, Luke tells us that Jesus returned to Galilee in **the power of the Spirit**. The Sonship anointing was fully activated.

THE POWER OF THE WILDERNESS

> Then Jesus returned in the power of the Spirit to Galilee, and news of Him went out through all the surrounding region. And He taught in their synagogues, being glorified by all. —Luke 4:14-15

To glean from His time in the wilderness, it is important to see these events *through the eyes of Jesus' experience.* **We are looking at the emergence of the last Adam—fulfilling what the first Adam could not.** Obviously, He realized something about manifesting His identity that as spiritual sons, we also need to know.

So, here's how we're going to view this. We will look through the lens of spirits, living in human bodies, deployed to Earth to manifest the power of the Kingdom as sons of God. And through this lens, we will not only see the Lord's time in the wilderness for what it really was; an appointed place of divine commissioning, instruction, and preparation for His Sonship manifestation. We will also see what and how we need to imitate Him, so that we too manifest our sonship identity.

We've established that the wilderness is not a divine punishment—I daresay that it also isn't always a dry, lonesome, isolated desert in the woods. You might live in a high-rise apartment, yet still be in the wilderness of Holy Spirit's choosing without ever leaving town. That's because we are talking about the solitary meeting place God sets aside for Himself to meet with you—setting the time, place, and duration. This is where we will train to know how to live according to the finished work of Heaven. The Holy Spirit leads us to a spiritual oasis to receive life-aligning corrections, instructions, and knowledge of how we will manifest the Kingdom of God in Earth.

Do you see that we have come to the place where our measure is taken, and our commitment level has been accessed? Here is when the noise of vaunting self-performance, pride, and flesh-exaltation dies, and the voice of the Father becomes the only one we even want to hear. The time to learn how to be mature sons is at hand—meaning those who are led by the Holy Spirit learn to live the sonship life that is sourced solely from Heaven. We seek the will of the Father, and obey the will of the King that we represent in all things. It's not just our true *"Come, Kingdom of God, be done, will of the King"* moment. It is also our *"Father, not my will, but only Your will is done"* transformation.

What do you suppose happened to Jesus in that holy convergence with the Father and Holy Spirit? I believe that this is the place where He mastered how to hear, see, live, and do on the Kingdom's level. He was now in the true Master class. This was different from every other time of solitude He had experienced. How can I say that? Because this was right after the Father had audibly and publicly confirmed His Sonship. I want to emphasize this point, because **it set Him on the intentional course of His fulfilled destiny —which is what we also seek to experience**.

In that solitary place, Jesus wasn't merely resisting temptation —He was being instructed on the protocols of the Kingdom—

THE POWER OF THE WILDERNESS

possibly even getting the lessons that the first Adam missed out on. This last Adam was instructed on how to live from the knowledge that comes through the tree of eternal life. He had no need to eat from or retain the knowledge of good and evil within Himself. He was being taught how to release royal dominion, and life-changing resurrection power by hearing, seeing, and doing only what the Father says. He did it as a spirit occupying a human body.

Some theologians say that He was a rabbi, others disagree, and the arguments abound on each side. Regardless, we know that He grew up in the ways of the Jewish religion, hearing the teachings and sermons taught in the temple. Those teachings were not just a release of religious rhetoric; these were the lifestyle instructions that declared how He was to live, think, believe, and conduct Himself as a Jew. As we pay attention to the words that He later spoke to the Pharisees, Sadducees, scribes, and others—you can see the way He had to separate from the traditional teachings to release the culture of God's Kingdom into the atmosphere.

MATTHEW'S GOSPEL SPEAKS ON HOW JESUS INSTRUCTED them in the ways of righteousness. He issued a lot of "You are..." statements as He taught. "You are blessed. You are the salt of the earth, and the light of the world." Then He told them, *"You have heard it was said, but I say to you..."* These were rebuttals to their traditional teachings. Can't you just see the Father and Spirit saying that to Him first? Then He went out and told others the same thing. **This is sonship identity in action!**

The Father's affirmation, *"This is My Son..."* solidified His identity and fortified His ability to obey. I believe it gave Him the impetus to pursue and develop a lifelong intimacy—He craved that time with Father more than food, sleep, or anything else. This revelation included more than just the knowledge that He was a King and Priest, the image and likeness of His Father. He also obtained the insights necessary to manifest His identity. Which means that **He learned the ways in which He was expected to represent *as* God in all things.**

In that sense, He was obligated to act like God, and wield the royal power of Heaven over the fish, birds, and every living thing moving on the earth. He had dominion over Earth itself, with the right to expect it to yield to His commands—which is why the wind and the waves bowed to the dominion of the King—everything was subject to His royalty, just as it had been in the genesis.

As a Son, Jesus learned obedience by what He experienced—every moment provided a divine instruction, all of which He obeyed. Can you see why He was constantly looking and listening, to see and hear what the Father wanted? Afterwards, He would do what He saw the Father doing *through Him*. That's why He could say, "The Father *in* Me does the works." He expected the Father to manifest what He showed the Son that He wanted to do. And all of these things are also part and parcel of our own sonship identity.*

Now let's look at what He was most likely instructed to do during these holy convergence sessions. Keep in mind, every instruction He received was tailored to His royal assignment. He had been deployed to the Earth to restore the Kingdom. Some say that He came to die. Yes, but He saw dying as a necessary step in the overall process to unleash His resurrection life power and our Kingdom spirit-sonship into Earth.

In order to do that, I believe that they had a number of strategic discussions during those forty days—fine tuning the details that made up the big picture. So it should not be a stretch to believe that the Father and Spirit coached the Son on how to continually manifest and never fail. He knew who He was—and they instructed Him on how to live the **"I Am/I Do"** identity while in His mortal body. It was like a call and response. Divine instruction led to internal declaration, then on to the outward manifestation of sonship identity. Throughout the gospels, we can see that these are some of the Heavenly protocols, the identifiers that Jesus lived by.

---

* See Hebrews 5:5-9; John 10:25, 38; 14:10-12.

OUR QUEST FOR IDENTITY

1. You are not ever offended.
2. You are not moved from your course.
3. You do not interpret a Spirit move through soul or physical understanding.
4. You think the way I do. See what I show you. Say what I say. Remain one with Me.
5. You are not led by your emotions. You do not harbor bitterness or anger.
6. You always give your emotions to Me in conversation and fellowship. Even in suffering wrong intentions, you've already chosen to release forgiveness.
7. What you hold within is what you are capable of releasing. Remain filled with My presence.
8. You are forgiveness. You are love. You are peace. Joy. Comfort. Anointed. Healer. Peace.
9. Always forgive. Your roots are in Me, not past actions and others' desires.
10. Stay debris free.
11. You are not obligated to cater to the whims of others. Your responsibility is to complete your assignment the way it is laid out before you.
12. Live *only* from what you superhumanly see and hear from Heaven.
13. Always look for My kingdom. You will always find it.
14. Your life is rooted in what you see through the eyes of the Spirit.

15. You operate in My royal power—that makes you the ruling Spirit everywhere that your feet tread.
16. You live by what the Father says concerning the things that you see, hear, and experience.
17. Talk to Me every day. All day.
18. Listen to Me always. (*Smith Wigglesworth said: "I hardly ever pray for more than twenty minutes, and I hardly ever go twenty minutes without prayer."*) This is Divine union and continual abiding.
19. Hear Me and do what I say.
20. Know that these are the Kingdom commands for living from the place of victory—because you will never lose a battle.

As we read through those twenty statements, the realization dawns. These are not confessions or affirmations. The same holds true for us. We also have **I am/I do** instructions. These are just a few of our key Kingdom identifiers—the manner by which we think, act, believe, do, and live as spirit-sons of God.

- I am not ever offended.
- I do not interpret life through the lens of emotions.
- I do not yield to or dwell on bitter memories.
- I always forgive.
- I think like the Father, see what He shows, and say what He says.

- I live from what is finished in Heaven, not from what appears on Earth.
- I always love.
- I walk by my Father's faith, not by earthbound sight.

There is no other option if we are to walk in the spirit-sonship power of God's Kingdom. **We do not emerge from the wilderness the same way we entered**. We are in our training season—so now is when we learn how, and then do. We learn to hear the voice of our Father as He wants to be heard. Every religious and ethnic filter is dismantled—we don't need the protection of ESD identity anymore. Our secular mindsets, family trauma, religious interpretations, political, social, and even business allegiances must all come into subjection to the way things are done in the Kingdom. Through our experiences, "we have heard it was said...." Now, through Jesus, the Father has given us this message: ***"but I SAY unto and through you...."***

HAVE YOU EVER WONDERED WHY SO MANY MINISTERS SET out to do the work of the ministry without first **looking to see** what the Father wants them to do, and how to do it? In part, it is because Heaven's way of thinking is not in place as **our only source of truth.** Some of us may believe that seeking God to obey Him is optional, especially if we think we already "know" the what and how of our calling. But revealed knowledge and visions from God come with instructions.

Another reason is that many operate solely on anointing, talents, and giftings. God entrusts us with His gifts of healing or wisdom, yet we work those gifts without building the character and maturity required to align with His Word. And possibly, because of our preexisting Christian ideology, we view the Kingdom of God message and sonship identity as optional or secondary to our doctrinal creeds or denominational positions, resulting in a form of godliness, but lacking in world-changing power.

True Kingdom power comes through the spirit-sons. The mind of Christ sets the standard for how we live, move, and have our "to be" identity. The body of Christ is not a bunch of societal martyrs or helpless survivors just holding on until we get beamed up, up, and away from this sin-filled, mean world. That's not how this works. **Sons of God do not run away from the works or manifestations of the devil.** We are here to be fruitful, multiply, fill and subdue the Earth, exercise Kingdom dominion over the territory, prosper through the release of Heaven's resources, and fulfill our assigned overcoming victory.

We speak the King's words to change the matters in this Earth, one sickness, disease, plague, circumstance, kingdom, mountain, or system at a time.* Our royal sonship mandate is

---

* See Genesis 1:26-28.

to manifest—allowing the truth of who and what we are to be seen in all of Earth. We are deployed here to govern as spirit-sons of God, ambassadors, citizens, servants, kings, and priests; and **the assignment will not change.** As we learn the royal protocols of true identity, the righteousness, peace, and joy of the Kingdom trains us to recognize and obey the will of our Father, meaning we get to trade our limitations for likeness.

Again, this is why the Son said only what the Father said. He is the express image and likeness of the Father. We are now manifested in His image and likeness—God's Sons on the Earth, contained in the Body of the One New Man. We are one body, one family with myriads of particles. Our unity and alignment is not with one another, it is with and in Him. Our quest for identity is not about individual promotion. It is about our emergence as the corporate son maturing into full expression. We grow up into all things into Him, and we suffer through the refiner's fire to come forth as gold.

Our time in the wilderness is marvelous, but **it is also self-confrontational**. Manifesting sonship identity is not just identifying, but also destroying our selfish choices of performance over obedience, platform over Presence, or busyness over intimacy. This is when and where we learn to overcome to the uttermost.

Jesus learned and then manifested obedience to the Father in everything. He had already been taught the principles and power of righteousness—but the actual experience of being righteous, overcoming temptation, betrayal, gossip, complaint, and team frustration had to be proven. His ability to overcome with the help of the Spirit of grace proves that we also overcome the same things with the same power and Helper. His crucifixion was absolutely necessary for us, but dying on the Cross in and of itself was **not the sole focus** of Jesus' assignment.

He came to restore the Kingdom that had been lost to us.* Our salvation and everything that followed is factored into the overall strategy. He had to get *past the crucifixion* and all of its torment and suffering in order for His name, blood, and stripes to be accounted as ransom. His blood was intentionally released into the Earth for a Kingdom purpose. It gave **evidence that a death had occurred, and a life had been given**. But if Calvary was where everything ended, we'd still be in bondage and ignorant of our sonship rights and responsibilities. Remember, Jesus prophesied and taught that He would die, spend three days in the earth, then He would rise up. But His emphasis was on *being* **The Resurrection.** He was excited about **the manifested power that He would unleash** as He looked beyond the shame of the cross. He saw the glory that the *"I Am The Resurrection and the Life"* would bring forth.†

> Keep your eyes on Jesus, who both began and finished this race we're in. Study how he did it. Because he never lost sight of where he was headed—that

---

* See Matthew 18:11, Luke 19:10.
† See John 11:21-27.

exhilarating finish in and with God—he could put up with anything along the way: cross, shame, whatever. And now he's there, in the place of honor, right alongside God. When you find yourselves flagging in your faith, go over that story again, item by item, that long litany of hostility he plowed through. That will shoot adrenaline into your souls! —Hebrews 12:2-3 MSG

Because Jesus finished His assignment, the outpouring of His blood on the Heavenly mercy seat manifested a spiritually legal, eternal transaction that restored the Kingdom on Earth, and activated our restored sonship identity, power, authority over sickness, disease, poverty, lack, and wholeness in the Kingdom. Sonship provides kingship, royal priesthood, image and likeness authority, eternal/resurrection life, unlimited dunamis grace power, heavenly languages, Kingdom possibilities. All things that pertain to life and godliness **have been given** to us. The Lord Jesus Christ manifested victory through His Sonship identity, and wants to show us how to go and do likewise. He's provided everything that we need.

It is time for us to do the same.

CHAPTER 23
THE FREQUENCY OF A GOD-CONTROLLED SPIRIT

> Sins's symptoms are sponsored by the senses, a mind dominated by the sensual. Thoughts betray source; spirit life attracts spirit thoughts.
>
> — ROMANS 8:5 THE MIRROR

Are you paying attention to who, what, and how you hear and speak? Jesus warned His disciples to *take heed of what* they heard, and of *how* they heard it.* *What we hear* speaks to the jurisdiction of our hearts. *How we hear* calls us to consider our degree of willingness to listen and understand His Kingdom ways. Inferred in that caution is the caveat to pay attention to who

---

* See Mark 4:24 and Luke 8:18.

or what you are listening to. Do we hear spirit and life words as spirit beings, or do we mute Kingdom words and ways, and turn up the volume on the earthly, sensual, devilish reasonings of our human emotions? Both admonitions speak to the condition of our hearts when God's words are given to us.

> **For the mind-set of the flesh is death, but the mind-set controlled by the Spirit finds life and peace.**
> —Romans 8:6 TPT

Prior to my total recognition of the familiar spirit of rebellion, I had another truth revealed to me pertaining to my former attitude toward obedience and reward. You see, for years I have been told that my financial wealth is connected to my obedience. I wondered why I had to obey every little thing to even get a decent monthly income, while a bunch of heathens and flaky church folks seemed to prosper in disobedience?

Because I measured obedience as a stumbling block, I missed what was intended to incentivize me—the blessings it brings. The realization that I resented God because He wanted me to do things His way is humbling. Of course, I didn't consciously admit that to myself or anyone else.

> **Thinking patterns are formed by reference; either the sensual appetites of the flesh and spiritual death, or zoe-life and total tranquility flowing from a mind addicted to spirit [faith] realities.** —Romans 8:6 Mirror

THE FREQUENCY OF A GOD-CONTROLLED SPIRIT

My mind was all twisted up in a knot of demonic assumptions of what it means to obey God. I resented the constant call to obedience, it *felt* like a punishment and control mechanisms being used against me. I *felt* as though God was using my body weight as a condition in a hostage negotiation, holding my income captive until we came to terms. I was at a loss as to how to negotiate its release. This was a demonstration of sheer ignorance. I had a rebellious heart—I did not want to be controlled, a sure sign of deception. That's one of the techniques demons use to influence humanity that life is better independent of God. **That's another lie.**

Let's apply a quantum mechanics perspective of observation, sound, vibration, and frequency to expand this understanding of controlling spirits. *How* I see, hear, and speak aligns with *what* I see, hear, and speak.

I observed **obedience** as a performance of works, viewing it as an outward task. I could have observed obedience to God as a spiritual weapon, which would have allowed me to see an inward strengthening power.

God's call to obedience is a release of sound waves calling His sons to manifest in the earth. The ways of the earth give over to the ways of the mind of Christ. You see, **to change from low Earth to Heaven-on-Earth frequencies**, we simply *change the origin of our thoughts, words, and actions.*

OUR QUEST FOR IDENTITY

To overcome is to **_always see oneself_** as one that defeats, bests, conquers, and vanquishes an opponent. The overcomer is the one that triumphs and prevails over obstacles, opponents, and the like, despite any disrupters. It's scriptural, you know, considering that Paul gives thanks to the God that always causes us to triumph in Christ, not because we're all that, but because He is.*

We are the people that enjoy success in all that we are obedient to do. Should you **dare to think, see, and believe** that overcoming is **all that you know how to do**, you **vibrate and manifest the frequency of an overcomer**—*even when a task is daunting*. You'll begin to think as a Heaven-sent spirit on assignment to overcome every demonic spirit on assignment against you. That's when you can see every weapon or assignment taking a position against you as a demonic spirit on a failed mission. We are created to resonate with Heaven—mature sonship frequencies vibrate obedience.

As I considered this possibility, the frequency of my mind changed, and I began to see a different picture. My sonship DNA is intended to resonate (or vibe) with all the ways of my Father—**because they are His ways**. We are originally created to obey God. It's part of our spiritual DNA, and it works from the internal to the outward me. The Spirit of God did not call me to modify my behavior.

---

* See 2 Corinthians 2:14-17.

THE FREQUENCY OF A GOD-CONTROLLED SPIRIT

He called me to switch to the resurrection life frequency of obedience that operates by the mind of Christ, so that I resonate as a Kingdom spirit-son in my female assigned dwelling place. Can you see what I'm saying? Look at how *The Mirror Bible Translation* opens up Romans 8:4-6:

> The very righteousness promoted by the law is now realized in us. Our practical day-to-day life bears witness to spirit inspiration and not flesh domination.
>
> ⁵Sin's symptoms are sponsored by the senses, a mind dominated by the sensual. Thoughts betray source; spirit life attracts spirit thoughts.
>
> ⁶Thinking patterns are formed by reference; either the sensual appetites of the flesh and spiritual death, or zoe-life and total tranquility flowing from a mind addicted to spirit [*faith*] realities.
>
> ⁷A mind focused on flesh (*the sensual domain where sin held me captive*) is distracted from with no inclination to his life-laws. Flesh [*self-righteousness*] and spirit [*faith righteousness*] are opposing forces. *(Flesh no longer defines you; faith does.)*
>
> ⁸It is impossible for those immersed in flesh to at the same time accommodate themselves to the opinion, desire and interest of God. *(The word aresko means to accommodate oneself to the opinions, desires and interests of others.)*

Years ago, a man named Robert Zimmerman, also known as the prolific composer/performer Bob Dylan, wrote and sang a song that proclaimed that no one is exempt in obeying or being the servant to one spirit or another, meaning either the Lord or the devil.[1]

The Spirit of God gave us the Kingdom key to manifest as His sons. Obedience to God is the identified lifestyle of the sons of God. Some might declare that they serve no one but themselves. That simply means that they rejected God.

You will definitely serve somebody. ***So, which kingdom have you chosen to serve?***

CHAPTER 24
OUR SONSHIP IDENTITY

But He said to me, "My grace is enough for you, for my power is made perfect in weakness..."

— 2 CORINTHIANS 12:9

Remember how God commanded the first royal couple to be fruitful, multiply, replenish, subdue and **exercise dominion** in the Earth? These Kingdom directives are the same as those in effect in **our *now*** time. So, as we're preparing to close this lesson, there is a vital issue we want to ensure that we have put into action. Simply stated, we must eliminate any tendency to tolerate sin as an acceptable behavior choice. Claiming that we're too weak to overcome a temptation is not just a compromise; it is a lie that must be removed from our respective mind scapes. Clearly, we are the people called by God to carry out the sonship mandate, so we must step into the fullness of our identity.

Why is this being said at the end of the book? Because some of us harbor the taste of fruit from the tree of the knowledge of good and evil, stubbornly refusing to allow the resurrecting zoe life power to manifest Kingdom dominion within our hearts. Sons of God operate from a position of certainty—there is no doubt about who our Father is, and how our Father wants things done, and no other way to live. Remember, the definition of the Kingdom of God is:

God's reign, His rule, His sovereignty.
His kingship, His rule, His authority.

The mind of Christ operates by revelation from the Spirit of Truth. We do not grow weary in our souls, and give up when life gets difficult. We endure chastening, correction, and discipline, as sons loved by our Father. We are being trained in such a way that we produce the fruit of peace and righteousness, just as Jesus showed us.* We have learned how our Father thinks, and how He wants things done, thus we have no other way of viewing hardship, betrayal, or any other assignment launched against us except as defeated. If we falter in this belief, it may be because we are still operating from the wrong kind of knowledge.

Let me say it plainly: we must shift from our concentrated

---

* See Hebrews 12:1-17.

study of the devil's ways of deception and lies to focus on increasing in our knowledge of the reality of the Kingdom that we come from. God has given us His spirit of power, love, and a sound mind. He trains and expects His sons to exercise dominion on Earth according to His word. Anything He wants us to know about the devil, He will tell us; otherwise, it is our responsibility to master the understanding of how Heaven works in the earth, and how His Spirit works through us. Our Father honestly wants us to learn to think beyond the limitations of a darkened understanding. Earthbound thinking is rooted in the expectation and attribution of things working or failing to work according to "common sense, fate, karma, or luck."

It's like what we see in Luke 5. Imagine being an experienced fisherman such as Simon Peter. You toil all night, and catch nothing. Then in daylight, Jesus tells you to launch out into deeper waters and throw your fishing nets on the other side of the boat—the side that common sense and experience says will not yield anything. Hmmm. Except, it does, because Jesus said to do it. Miraculous? Yes, yet to Jesus, this was simply an example of how a Son exercises Kingdom dominion over the fish.

Everyone else thinks that the fish dictate when they will be caught, so the earthbound mind says, *"It won't work."* That's not the mind a son of God thinks or acts from. The sonship mind operates in miracle-working power and authority as part of the Kingdom directives. Miracles have not passed away, son of God. And they don't all happen through one or two name brand ministers at big camp meetings. *Miracles are supposed to happen through you, too.* Think about that.

To help expand my vision and allow His mind to move me outside of the typical earthbound thinks, the Holy Spirit led me to begin using *what if* query exercises. My original concept of how this *what if* query came about five years ago, after reading Pastor Tommy Barnett's book, *What If*. On occasion my mom and apostle, Dr. Bacer J. Baker, voluntells our congregation to read certain books. *What If* was one of them. *Thank you, Mommy.*

So I posit to you, ***what if*** you thought about your life and every situation solely operating within and from the sonship mind of Christ?

- ***What if*** you began to explore life with that mind to see Kingdom possibilities everywhere you've looked in despair?
- ***What if*** you allowed yourself to be Spirit-led into the wilderness of His choosing, then took advantage of your opportunity to ask God the questions that He designed you to ask Him?
- ***What if*** you believed what He said about you to the point that you *become* everything He said that you are?
- ***What if*** you realized that these things are entirely

within your scope of doing, because that's precisely what sons of God do to manifest?
- **What if** you chose to live according to the tree of life, rejecting intimate knowledge of good and evil?

WE'VE REACHED THE CLOSING MINUTES OF OUR QUEST— the altar call moment when you and I make the choice to stand or sit, fight or fold, hide or reveal, change or stay the same, overcome or be defeated. A number of the issues in life and common temptations we all face have been brought to your attention. I've shared about my graveyard-style grief, tombs of torment and self-inflicted cuttings.

You've heard about my rebellious, disobedient posture, and even witnessed aspects of a glorious deliverance from familiar spirits that plagued me since childhood. You've witnessed how my personal experiences have led me to asking the Holy Spirit the type of questions that are prompted by Him so that He can give me the answers I have needed. The queries still seemed to come in moments when weakness is louder than strength, and things look hopeless.

That's when He posited solutions or escape strategies that overrode the futility and pain of each situation. If you allow truth to bear witness; my stories, breakthroughs, and deliverances should have also highlighted parallel scenarios in your life. Undoubtedly, I have shared more than enough about the pattern of spiritual disrupters and broken pieces stemming from my childhood and adult life to stir your own memories and prompt your own dialogue with the Holy Spirit.

FOR THE PAST TWO YEARS, I HAVE BEEN LEARNING HOW to seek Kingdom insights from the Holy Spirit by using the series of questions that He taught me to ask Him. The toughest one: *"What does my life look like **if I think, believe, and live** as one that had never been raped? Molested? Abused? Thrown away? Devalued? Defiled? Divorced?*

Notice, I **did not say** as though it did not happen. All of these things DID happen to me. But ***what if*** I recognize that as a son of God, **I am equipped with the grace power to live beyond the disrupters?** Because I am one that is realigned to the will of my King, **how will I think? How *do* I think? Speak? Act? Believe?**

It has taken almost six months for me to really hear His response to these questions. Partially because the rebellious part of my soul I told you about did not want to allow me to look at Kingdom possibilities. Remember that question, ***"What if I recognized that as a son of God, I am equipped to live beyond the demonic disrupters?"***

As I've shared, I could not see that as being true, so I've flailed about in a pit of indecision. Incredibly, part of His response to me was the instruction to go back to writing this particular book. When I tell you that the book I originally wrote under this title is not what you've read, I am so understating the facts.

He gave me the solution when I asked the breakthrough question He gave me to ask. I needed increased capacity to apply the answer that He gave me back then. It has taken this journey with you to be able to see what I could or would not see before—what you and I all need to understand.

It is when we're done with the graveyards and tombs of trauma—done with the self-abuse, the pigs, and the unclean spirits torments— and we run to Jesus, falling at His feet in worship—that's when we are ready to be clothed in His righteous mind.

YOU ARE EXHORTED TO BEGIN SEEING THE *"WHAT IF'S"* *of life* as Holy Spirit-led queries pointing to your opportunity to envision the heavenly possibilities assigned to work for and through you. Allow these questions to open your ears, eyes, hearts, and lips to hear, see, embrace, and speak forth the vision, dreams and "on Earth as in Heaven" Kingdom realities that God reveals from the *"It is finished"* place.

These queries are intended to cause our hearts to expand in the capacity to know God as **our only Source** for everything. What was once only viewed as impossible, we get to see through the eyes of our Father, **the God of all things possible**. This is the foundation of Kingdom 101 sonship identity. The King of king's plans, hopes and dreams are imaged in, then through us.

Imagine. Jesus believed **every word** that the Father told Him, so when He told His followers that with God all things are possible, **Jesus believed what He said**. These spirit and life, *on Earth as in Heaven,* words do not return to God until He fulfills them through us. What else do you suppose His belief in God's Word released? He released spirit and life sparks of light—not mere words—but living spirit lifelines of Kingdom power that supercharge Earth's atmosphere every time an obedient son of God speaks the King's will. I've begun to see this as a reality.*

Another thing that Jesus, the first begotten Son released is the image and likeness mantle that authorizes us, as born-from-above spiritual sons of God to believe and behave in the same manner that He did. The mysteries of the Kingdom really have been given to us to know, believe, become, and release; because once again, the righteousness and dominion power of the Kingdom can be wielded through the utterance and actions of the true sons of God.

Sonship is your identity. By now, you should be very clear on that. *What ifs* bring forth the something said, that which is already so, from the timeless domain of *all things possible*. As He reveals the answers to our *What if* questions, we are prepared to move on to the next phase. *What if* opens

---

* See John 6:63 - He released the Spirit life through His spoken words!

the door to possibilities. Our next step, *"Because I am... therefore I do..."* takes us across the threshold. You now know who and what you are. For Jesus, that happened in the wilderness of Heaven's choosing.

I am happy to declare that this quest has led me to the answers that I have so desperately desired. The encounters I've experienced with the Lord are to His liking, different from any I've had before. Along with many of you, I knew that I am a son of God, but had need to learn just what being a spirit-son, image, likeness, king, and priest looks like in me.

During this journey, I caught brief glimpses of a wilderness-time set aside for me, the place where full understanding of how to manifest my sonship awaits. I think you can guess what is currently on His agenda for me, if not I'll tell you.

I've taken the challenge He set before me, to learn how to manifest as an overcomer of spiritual disrupters, and allow Him to introduce me to the reality of being one that lives free of the traumas of yesterday. I know this is possible, because Jesus and His blood has already made it my reality. I have been led into the wilderness of my sonship identity, and I love what I've discovered thus far. I pray the same for you.

Some of you have crossed the threshold. You've begun to speak with certainty, *"I know that I am a son. I'm ready to learn how to take action according to the sonship pattern laid out by Jesus."* And that is an entirely new lesson. You may need to read this book again, and possibly a third time, working through each section. As for me, I have more to

OUR QUEST FOR IDENTITY

unlearn and learn, and I will continue to do so as I enjoy my time with Him in the wilderness of discovery. And yes, I expect to come forth in the dunamis power of the Holy Spirit, according to the sonship pattern.

The Kingdom progression is established: Spirit, Son, Image, Likeness, King, Priest, Citizen, Ambassador, Influencer, and on it goes. Here's your final question on this *Quest for Identity*.

> **Will you enter your wilderness to manifest Kingdom spiritual sonship or will you remain an orphaned counterfeit?**

I believe that you, like me, answered **"Kingdom."** If I'm right, then you will also do what you must to be ready for the next phase of our ***Kingdom 101 Foundations*** journey. I am quite excited about what I see ahead. What do I see? I'm glad you asked. The stirrings of manifestation, of course. Together we'll explore that terrain as we take on the **Level Two Challenge**, to experience *Sonship In Action*, the next book in this series.

That's all for now. I declare the blessings of the Lord truly do manifest in your life. I love you.

Class dismissed.

OUR SONSHIP IDENTITY

PART III
APPENDICES

APPENDIX A

LEXICON OF POSSIBILITIES, INQUIRIES, AND DISCOVERY (SELECTED ENTRIES)

Assumptive understanding is well-known as a communication issue, when a spoken or written word does not always convey the same meaning to its hearers and readers. Our definitions of words are often shaped by our own experiences, understandings, and interpretations, which can lead to differences in interpretation. That never works when trying to comprehend spiritual matters in the Kingdom of God, where the Creator King Himself defines His own words.

For this reason, I have begun compiling this Lexicon of insights gleaned from the Word of God. We will use it throughout the five books in this series—so you may find words listed here that are not in the manuscript that you're studying. They may have been cut during edits, but the phrases are still viable. This is an ongoing work, a growing collection of my own Kingdom inquiries, propositions of possibilities, and discoveries of how to manifest what I

APPENDIX A

discover. It is crafted for those who seek not only knowledge but also revelations and impartations. Each word in this Lexicon is intended to open a door to deeper Kingdom understanding, formed at the intersection of scripture, theology, scholarly, linguistic, and prophetic insight. I want to go beyond mere definitions, and cross thresholds into royal protocols and insights, the language of seekers, reformers, scribes, and sons.

Activator Mechanism (n.) The Kingdom mechanism by which unseen truth becomes seen. Not a creative force itself, but the spiritual pull that draws the finished work from eternity into present visibility. Often paired with quantum faith®.[1]

Disrupter (n.)

1. A supernatural force that dismantles, interrupts, or overrides an existing system, either to enforce divine order or to establish disorder. (*Genesis* 1:3, 2 *Corinthians* 10:4)
2. A divine intervention that causes the collapse of carnal or kosmos-based cycles.
3. A spiritual being or spoken word sent to dismantle demonic infrastructures.
4. A mental, spiritual, or genetic interference that alters perception, belief, or behavior—either through divine transformation or traumatic imprinting. (*Romans* 12:2, *Exodus* 20:5)
5. A cycle breaker—one who disrupts patterns of

oppression, deception, or limitation to establish Kingdom reality.
6. A force of Kingdom light that unseats darkness through sudden, catalytic truth.
7. Spiritually speaking: contextual keywords for *disrupter* include: divine intervention, change of frequency, time, or outcome, cosmic alteration, mental assault, demonic interference, traumatic experience, and the effect of spiritual laws, i.e., sin and death, knowledge of good and evil, spirit of life in Christ Jesus.

Etymology (n.) Derived from Old French *questa* and Latin *quaerere* (to seek, inquire, ask).*

Frequency (n.) Range of sonship power (spiritual sound waves) released into the spiritual atmosphere when speaking, thinking, believing, and releasing words. Determines the degree and weight of power and authority recognized by the Earth, and the demonic realm. *Low-frequency range is shown in Acts 19:11-20 with the sons of Sceva, who operated at the low-frequency level of hearsay, instead of from true intimacy with the power of the Name of Jesus.*

Oral Tradition (n.) From the Latin *tradere*, "to hand over" or "to transmit." In the Kingdom context, oral tradition is not simply a method of passing on information—it is a sacred mode of impartation. Oral tradition carries breath,

---

* Webster's 1828 Dictionary.

cadence, covenant, and spirit. It preserves identity and mystery by voice, long before ink and page.

OTS - Oral Tradition Storyteller (n.) A modern-day Kingdom scribe (writer/teacher) who operates within the cadence of oral transmission while writing, teaching, or preaching. The OTS preserves the ancient flame of story, honor, scroll, and Spirit. This voice does not merely inform—it reforms. The OTS operates in a prophetic rhythm, often releasing revelation through layered narrative, metaphor, and poetic cadence.

Parables (n. pl.) Symbolic narratives used by Jesus and others throughout Scripture to encode Kingdom mysteries within story. Parables function as both mirror and map—reflecting the heart while guiding the seeker deeper. Though elusive in definition, their purpose is divine provocation.

Physics-to-Faith Parallel (n.) The correspondence between natural laws and supernatural Kingdom authority. Used to contrast faith's governing capacity with the constraints of physics—such as Archimedes' principle (buoyancy) vs. Jesus walking on water. Faith suspends or overrides natural law through spiritual dominance.

Posit (n.) An expression of truth put forth for testing; rooted in a belief so deeply established in divine origin that it stands immovable, even when unseen. Posits are Holy Spirit led inquiries of Heaven, standards that defy the impossible limitations of life; earthbound beliefs that once challenged by truth, are led to yield in submission to Kingdom-governed reality.

Possibility (n.) A quantum opening for divine manifestation of Kingdom of God reality. Possibilities respond to faith-infused speech rooted in eternal truths.

Quantum Faith ® **(n.)** This phrase, based upon faith principles that are demonstrated through quantum mechanics, was coined by Annette Capps. Both the phrase and the teaching of these actions can be found in her book of the same name.[2] The activator mechanism by which sons of God collapse unseen realities into the seen world. It is the alignment of spirit, mind, and mouth with the eternal Word, issuing a timestamped decree that brings the timeless into the now. This faith speaks from finished truth and enforces its manifestation into physical matter.

Quest (n.)

A series of questions that begins and leads one to embark upon a journey of sonship discovery.

To ask specific questions in fulfillment of a royal summons, then journey and find the answers and solutions necessary to manifest Heaven's solutions on Earth according to the desires of our King.

A journey or pursuit driven by an initial question, undertaken to seek, discover, or achieve a goal, calling, unresolved inquiry, or true identity. *Example: My quest for identity*

APPENDIX A

begins with a single question—what do I need to do to manifest as a true mature son?

A Kingdom of God query or sacred search that begins when a "*What if?*" merges with heavenly finished realm possibilities in the act of searching or investigating. Typically in response to curiosity, doubt, or the pursuit of deeper understanding sought from the council of the Holy Spirit.

(Archaic) A formal, noble or adventurous expedition, made in response to a royal decree or internal summons. Often associated with a chivalric or mythological pledge or vow.

Time stamping (v.) The prophetic act of declaring the **now**-time of an eternal truth. It pulls a finished reality from the unseen into present manifestation. Time stamping marks the moment when divine reality is summoned from future unseen into NOW time.

APPENDIX B
NOTES & CITATIONS: STUDY RESOURCES: ARTICLES, AUTHORS, & WEBSITES

Needless to say, a lot of research, reading, and study went into the stories and traditions shared in this book. Listed in this appendix are a number of the resources, websites, and other materials that were not footnoted. Not all citations, sources, and linguistic bridges were quoted, but some of you may find my scholarly journey of interest. This section serves as scholarly trail markers, illuminating the path that others have trodden to assist us as we make way for others.

Annette Capps. *Quantum Faith* (Broken Arrow, OK: Capps Publishing, 2004).

Anthony A. Hoekema. *Created in God's Image* (Eerdmans, 1986). A foundational theological study on *Imago Dei* from a Reformed but accessible perspective. Hoekema explores spirit-soul-body unity, dominion, and restoration in Christ.

APPENDIX B

Graham A. Cole. *Faithful Theology: An Introduction* (Crossway, 2020). Contains an excellent summary of *Imago Dei* within the framework of divine revelation and humanity's role as image-bearers.

Geldenhuys, Norval. *The Gospel of Luke.* The New International Commentary on the New Testament. Reprint, Grand Rapids: Wm. B. Eerdmans Publishing Co., 1988. ISBN 0-8028-2184-7.

Harris, R. Laird, Gleason L. Archer Jr., and Bruce K. Waltke, eds. *Theological Wordbook of the Old Testament.* Chicago: Moody Press, 1980. s.v. "6754 192 ",צֶלֶם . https://archive.org/details/theologicalwordboooounse_n9s9

Jacob Neusner. *Genesis Rabbah: The Judaic Commentary to the Book of Genesis.* Atlanta: Scholars Press, 1985. https://archive.org/details/genesisrabbahjud0001unse

Jeff A. Benner. "Hebrew Words for 'Image'." *Ancient Hebrew Research Center.* Accessed March 22, 2025. https://www.ancient-hebrew.org/studies-words/hebrew-words-for-image.htm

Klyne Snodgrass. *Stories with Intent: A Comprehensive Guide to the Parables of Jesus*, 2nd ed. (Grand Rapids: Eerdmans, 2018), 7.

Nahum M. Sarna. *Genesis: The Traditional Hebrew Text with the New JPS Translation.* Philadelphia: Jewish Publication Society, 1989. https://books.google.com/books?id=BX2dNwAACAAJ

APPENDIX B

Michael Filimowicz. "The Quantum Divine: When Science Becomes the Gateway to the Spiritual," *Medium*, accessed March 22, 2025, https://medium.com/quantum-psychology-and-engineering/the-quantum-divine-when-science-becomes-the-gateway-to-the-spiritual-42a6833c367a.

Michael Heiser. *What Does It Mean to Be Made in the Image of God?* (BibleProject, essay/booklet form). Heiser brings insight into functional and relational views of *Imago Dei* based on Hebrew context.

BibleProject.org – *"Image of God"* Word Study. https://bibleproject.com. This site provides rich visual and textual exploration of *tselem* and *demut*. Great for readers who want a narrative + visual unpacking.

GotQuestions.org – *"What Is the Image of God?"* https://www.gotquestions.org/image-of-God.html. This site provides visitors with a basic evangelical overview; useful for readers seeking clear, entry-level explanation.

Theopedia.com – *"Image of God"* Entry https://www.theopedia.com/image-of-god. Includes short encyclopedic-style summaries with theological citations.

APPENDIX C
THE ANCIENT HEBREW MIND [EXCERPTS FROM "THE ANCIENT HEBREW LEXICON OF THE BIBLE"]

According to Jeff Benner, author of the *Ancient Hebrew Lexicon of the Bible* (*AHLB*), the Hebrew language was originally written with a pictographic script similar to Egyptian hieroglyphs. When Israel was taken into Babylonian captivity they adopted and used the Aramaic script of the region to write Hebrew. As we read through the Old Testament, we need to understand that the **ancient** Hebrew language is a concrete-oriented language, thus the meaning of Hebrew words in our Bibles are rooted in descriptive things we can see, taste, smell, hear, or touch.[1]

As readers of Biblical text, first and foremost, the concept we must learn and remember is of the culture of origin. The Hebrews of the Old Testament were people of an ancient near eastern culture, while most that read this book are likely

APPENDIX C

of a western cultural mind. By the inspiration of God,* the Hebrew writers communicated to those *of the same culture*, using examples, idioms, figures of speech, phrases, etcetera that were familiar and easily recognizable to them. The Word of God is our foremost resource in our ordained quest for identity. As we learn and gain understanding of the cultural mind and thought processes of these historical people, our understanding of God's mind and His ways will increase through the scriptural text that we read.

---

* 2 Timothy 3:15

APPENDIX C

REENA'S QUEST

The Mists of Duperie

REENA'S QUEST: THE MISTS OF DUPERIE

EXCERPTS FROM REENA'S QUEST BY LONZINE LEE (COPYRIGHT 2025).

Reena Hunter, college student and, according to her parents, "princess of the united kingdoms of Bastion and Papillon," found herself in a state of perplexity. First, that itchy feeling like she was being watched. She could feel eyes on her everywhere she went, but saw no one, which was not totally unusual, not with the parents she had.

But this was different—because she normally didn't notice. Then there were those weird dreams with all the mysterious voices calling to her. Last night's was the strangest one yet. Definitely, this was not the best of days. Thankfully, the answering text came back from her friend, Wen'ah.

> Let's meet.

Yes! Time to get to town and see if she could make any sense out of this crazy day. Grabbing her helmet and keys from the table, she whistled for Mieelo, her mini German Shepherd, pocketed her phone, and headed out the door.

Preoccupied though she was, Reena still noted the gloom of the day, and the absence of noise so typical for early morning. Usually the grounds were a hub of activity. Where was everyone? They must have had an early start, or they were all in a staff meeting. It happened. Trotting beside her, Mieelo was also watchful, sniffing the air as though searching for something he smelled, but did not see. Although he didn't alert, he remained watchful as he hopped into his carrier on Shadow, her pet name for her sleek, black, futuristic sport cycle.

Fastening him in place, she mounted her seat, passed her hand over the touch ID screen and hit the starter button. Usually she smiled at the purr of power, but at the moment she was more aware of the weighty atmosphere, somewhat hushed and anticipatory. Gazing around the empty grounds and courtyard, nothing appeared out of place. True, the unusual silence, coupled with the peculiar shadows that seemed to hover nearby, could have been cause for concern. However, she felt no threat or sense of unease. In fact, the shadows felt almost friendly. But as she circled around the driveway and through the gates, again she had the sense of eyes watching her.

The private road from their hilltop castle was a biker's dream. With its curves and sharp turns, it normally only took a few minutes to descend to the main road towards town. *But today* continued to be a different kind of day, one in which a continual series of sudden events would take precedence over the norm.

Midway down the mountain, a curious mist of swirling dust particles suddenly rose from the ground, meeting her in the middle of the road. Too late to swerve or even brake, she drove straight through, and that's when weird became weirder still. Because the regular road disappeared, and Reena found herself set upon an eerily lit crossroad, one that was not usually there. At least, she'd never seen it before. And Reena knew every side trail in her domain.

Braking to a stop…Shadow's engine purred in the silence. *What the heck!* She whipped her head backwards, but nothing was there. *Was that thing waiting for me?* Straddling the bike, Reena turned her head back, fighting against panic. Her heart rapidly thrummed against her chest, her adrenaline shot to a peak and breathing was suddenly a problem. Strangely, Mieelo didn't react. His huffing and soft whimper gave her comfort, as did the feel of his muzzle against her back. *"We're okay, boy. We're okay."* Relaxing her tightened grasp on the bars, she reached up and removed her helmet, then bent her head to her chest to slow her breathing. *"We're okay. I'm okay."*

Raising her head a few moments later, her puzzled gaze taking in the quiet surroundings. It looked like she had driven directly into the center of a parallel set of woods. Seated as she was, facing a forest of sorts, her straddled feet were firmly planted, one on each side. She looked at the tall, lush trees on her right, lined in a path as far as her eyes could see; to her left, equally lush but paler trees did the same thing. And the crossed roads were strange too; pavement on one side, but a dirt path on the other, and they were lit differently, like two different time zones. *"Where are we?"*

From her vantage point, she could see that the left side looked really old. Older than, hmmm—if she was seeing right—it was almost like the trees and paths were from different times. Even the soils were different. And **was that a sword stuck in a tree stump?** The realization was so startling, she forgot to be afraid. *"A sword? I've got to see this."*

Prepping her dismount, she steered Shadow toward the left. As she did, the still idling engine suddenly powered down and cut off. Then her touch screen went black…she reached into her leg bag pocket—and, yeah. Her phone went dark. Wow, the dust thing was bad enough, but this? She knew that Shadow was in top condition. It was a prototype, and the castle maintenance crew was very meticulous when it came to her equipment. So why did the engine just cut off? Reena desperately needed to be on time, to talk to Wen'ah. She was never late for appointments. But this…enchanted forest or whatever kind of mystical crossroad thing she faced *definitely* did not lead back to town.

Mieelo whined his urgent whine, the sound loud in the eerie silence. Kicking the stand in place, she dismounted, then let him down to do his thing, slipping her helmet strap onto her shoulder. As she moved closer to the stump, she was sure that she'd never seen this place before. *"Maybe I came through a time portal."* She chuckled to herself, then sighed. *"What am I going to do?"* **And that stopped her in her tracks as snippets of her dream came back to her mind.**

REENA'S QUEST: THE MISTS OF DUPERIE

Stay small. Stay safe. The familiar litany played through the corridors of young Reena's mind as she hid under the bedcovers. She could see the shadow wisps swirling around the air. They looked like musical notes floating in the air, and they were singing:

"Find your key. Use your key, Princess.
The scrolls of wisdom speak.
It is time. It is time. It is time.

You must find your key
and come into the first portal.
The key is found at the crossroad of your mind."

SCROLLS OF WISDOM? THE KEY TO THE FIRST PORTAL? WHAT IN EARTH WERE THEY TALKING ABOUT?

"You have the key. Use your key, Princess.
Begin the journey.
Time to see what you're meant to be.
Come and see. Come and see."

AND THEN, A DIFFERENT VOICE...

"Reena, before your thoughts can be in sync with the Sar Ruach, brain debris must be discarded...the mists that seek you desire to persuade you with what you should never desire."

Okayyy. Yes, she definitely needed to talk to Wen'ah. With both parents out of town, her advisor was the next best thing. But first, she needed to figure out how to get out of wherever she was. She stood, looking away from the tree stump to look for Mieelo, who hadn't returned to her side after taking care of business. There he sat, directly in the middle of the two paths, looking up with an attentive tilt of his head, as though he was receiving instructions from someone.

"Stay small. Stay safe." She'd spoken those same words to herself many times over the years... ...but for the first time, she allowed counter thoughts to rise up. The invitation was intriguing. Keys and portals and mists sounded like a mystical quest. Like the stories she probably read too often. Of course she knew who Sar Ruach was, but not what was meant by being in sync with Him. And then she heard it, the voice from her dreams.

> *"Be synchronized and set*
> *To the ebb and flow*
> *of the King's breath.*
> *"Princess Reena. This is your story.*
> *This is your time. Come on the journey.*
> *Come and see.*
> *The timeless truth reveals your key."*

What's safe, anyway? To consider following those dream words went against every thought she held since she saw.... *Or do those thoughts hold you?* There! That was the question.

"I'm so sick and tired of making these 'safe' decisions. What if I do pick something different?" She stomped her foot as she growled in frustration. Mieelo perked up his ears, looking to the left, emitting a low warning growl deep from his chest. Just like that he moved from relaxed to alert. His hackles raised, gaze fixed on something beyond the old stump to the trees along the old pathway.

"What is it, Mieelo? Do you know how we can get out of this mess?" He growled again, gaze still fixed on the path on the old woods side. Following his gaze, Reena heard it before she saw it. What looked like a small smoky, misty formation was drifting among the old trees. *"That wasn't there before."* She stepped over toward Mieelo.

Ding. Ding. Her cell phone trilled an incoming text. How weird was that? No GPS, but a text comes through? Looking at the screen, the message from Wen'ah, her friend and mentor flashed up in a pale gray bubble.

> Heading to the cafe.

Mieelo stood at attention, his growl, followed by three sharp barks startled her with its intensity. She looked back toward the path. What! The mist had grown larger...and louder. What's more, it was closer than before. *"Okay, time to move, Mieelo."* He turned around and jumped up into his carrier.

She jumped astride Shadow and kicked up the stand, relieved to see the touch screen flicker on as she passed her hand over its face, tried a jump start...and it worked! Releasing and putting on her helmet in practiced movements, she dared a look behind her. Oh my! The mist was at the stump. Turning back, she peeled away, back the way they came, not even surprised when the dust particles kicked up again. She just roared straight through.

Behind them, the hungry mist halted abruptly at the edge of the divide, roiling and hissing in a swirling vortex of vaporous coils. It could go no further. Cacophonous shrieks of frustration and rage reverberated through the air, creating an inhuman, shrill scream in the otherwise silent woodland.

Surprisingly, Reena reached the edge of town right on time. It was like that detour never happened. Just another weird happening in a very strange day. Sitting in a chair near the main wall of the pet-friendly café, watching Mieelo enjoy his pup cup, she smiled as she thought of an old movie line. *"Portals, and dreams, and mists. Oh my."* Reena's smile widened in relief as she watched the approach of her advisor and friend. Boy, did they have some things to discuss.

Wen'ah, diminutive in stature, beautiful in appearance, powerful in battle, typically turned heads when she walked into a room. Today was no exception. *"Wen'ah! I am so glad to see you!"* Rising to greet her, Reena was startled by the strength of Wen'ah's hands upon hers, and the tiny earbuds and recorder she pressed into her palms, holding onto her as they locked gazes.

"No time for pleasantries, Princess. I have some news that you urgently need to hear, it's on this recorder. We have a short

journey to take. We've received an alert. Your safety is compromised. There's an old family friend who can help you. The time has come for you to meet. Let's go. We'll take my truck. You can put Shadow in the back." And out the door she went, knowing Reena would follow.

Dramatic much? Yet, Wen'ah's words were strangely comforting, necessary after her crazy morning. Finally, a plan. My safety? An old friend? She had a lot of questions, but it had been instilled in her to follow instructions without hesitation, so she followed her out the café, Mieelo by her side. She knew the answers would come, but more prominent right now was the resounding question in Reena's mind. *"Stay safe."* She would not be alone. *"What if I dare to believe..?"* And strangely, she recalled the words that her mother, Nessa, spoke so often. ***It always begins in the forest.***

Placing Mieelo in the cage Wen'ah kept in the back of the cab just for him, she rolled Shadow up the ramp and secured the wheels into place. The pull to venture upon this dream quest growing inside of her, the picture of a secluded forest cabin flashed in her mind's eye as she settled in her seat. Her father's favorite getaway place. She suddenly knew where they were going, without Wen'ah saying a word. No GPS necessary. *"I guess it really does begin in the forest..."* Her quest was begun.

BEWARE OF THE SKOTOS!

The Skotos are darkness in motion, one of the creatures that live and move in the Zophos—what some refer to as *The Myriad of Mists*, for there is not just one. Nay, there are many breeds of the mists. Skotos are bred there with the sole function to trick living beings into granting them host access.

Skotos are part of the Zophos. Their specialized evil is to envelop the lives of humans. They are maskers, suffocating human minds through the words they are enticed into speaking. They hail from the *Mists of Duperie*, using deception and trickery to wrap human minds in veils of foolish distraction. Distraction provides entrance, which is how Skotos are able to slowly ooze into human minds. They feed upon hopes and dreams within them, until they completely consume their vitality, in preparation for the soul feeders. Feasting on human souls is the nature of the Nephos. **You Must Beware Of Them, Too.**

Somewhere between the portals of Eterna and Ehrets is a twisted land of deception, darkness and volatile, treacherous activity. It is more commonly known as *The Myriad of Mists,* the otherworldly lair of denizens of destruction. Contrary to its name, some of the mists are compellingly beautiful, vaporous traps. Many humans are tempted to cross over... then cannot escape. Only the sons of Sar Ruach possess the wisdom and power to exit at will.

REENA'S QUEST: THE MISTS OF DUPERIE

****

The Key That Unveils The Mystery Has Been Given To You.

Το κλειδί που αποκαλύπτει το μυστήριο σας έχει δοθεί.

You just met Reena and Wen'ah on the eve of their great adventure. We look forward to sharing more of their story as well as providing glimpses into the lives of the other men and women found in the annals of ***The Spirit Warrior Trilogy.***

EXCERPTS FROM REENA'S QUEST BY LONZINE LEE (COPYRIGHT 2025).

****

ENDNOTES

1. THE PURPOSE OF IDENTITY

1. I didn't attribute the phrase "Light, come forth" to a specific source, as it came to me through prayer while writing this chapter. However, I later found it used in an online verse-by-verse exegesis of Genesis 1:1-2:4 by Benjamin Brodie. You can find it here: https://versebyverse.com/background.html.
2. Merriam-Webster.com Dictionary, s.v. "identity," accessed May 12, 2025, https://www.merriam-webster.com/dictionary/identity.
3. Genesis 1:28, paraphrased, with a sprinkling of 2 Peter 1:1-15.
4. This definition of Kingdom is taken from George Eldon Ladd, *The Gospel of The Kingdom* (Grand Rapids, MI: Eerdmans, 1959), 19-23.

3. THE WEAPONS OF THEIR WARFARE

1. Yes, there were female knights, warriors, and women of many nations that led troops into heroic battle. While typically known as women of valor, or even "Dames" in England, the emphasis was not on their gender, but their historical accomplishments of skill, shrewd strategies, and bravery. Although never knighted, Joan of Arc is one of many such examples. "Female Knights of the Middle Ages," Amazing Women in History, accessed June 17, 2025, https://amazingwomeninhistory.com/female-knights-of-the-middle-ages/.
2. Spoils are regarded as the rewards, plunder, or gain of warfare, including valuables such as jewels, silver, gold, territory, property, goods, livestock, and in some instances, even people. Scriptural examples can be found in Joshua 7, Judges 5, and 1 Chronicles 26 to name a few.
3. Excerpts from The 'souled' flesh: Beyond mind-body dualism [1] Daniel Esparza, published on 08/21/24, https://aleteia.org/2024/08/21/the-souled-flesh-beyond-mind-body-dualism. Bold emphasis mine.

ENDNOTES

5. THE CORE ASPECTS OF OUR IDENTITY

1. These named are just a few that I watched, listened to, or read as I was writing this book. Honestly, I have quite a number of others. There is a list of some of their books or online teachings in Appendix B, *Notes & Citations* at the end of the book.
2. In Hebrew, the word for "image" is צֶלֶם (*tselem*), meaning a shadow, reflection, or imprint of divine essence. "Likeness" is דְמוּת (*demut*), which refers to resemblance not merely in form, but in function and operation—a spiritual blueprint for how we are to govern and move like our Creator. The Aramaic counterpart צַלְמָא (*tsalma*), used in similar ancient texts, affirms this truth. Regardless of the language we use, the truth remains. We were fashioned to bear God's nature and reflect His presence on earth.

    Imago Dei is the Latin phrase, Image of God. We'll further this discussion in Chapter 8, *The Image & Likeness Influence*.

7. THE HEART OF THE KING

1. Cf. *Isaiah 40:22* ("He stretches out the heavens like a curtain and spreads them out like a tent to dwell in"), *Psalm 103:19* ("The Lord has established His throne in the heavens, and His Kingdom rules over all"), *Colossians 1:17* ("In him all things hold together"), and *Hebrews 11:3* ("By faith we understand the ages to have been prepared by a saying of God, in regard to the things seen not having come out of things appearing;"), all quotations adapted from ESV, NEB and YLT for flow and clarity.

8. THE IMAGE & LIKENESS INFLUENCE

1. Jeff A. Benner, *Ancient Hebrew Lexicon of the Bible* (College Station, TX: Virtualbookworm.com Publishing, 2005).
2. *Theological Wordbook of the Old Testament* (TWOT): Harris, R. Laird, Gleason L. Archer Jr., and Bruce K. Waltke, eds. *Theological Wordbook of the Old Testament*. Chicago: Moody Press, 1980, 1:192, s.v., דְמוּת (demuth)".

9. THE IMAGO DEI: FROM MOSES TO JESUS TO YOU

1. Peter Enns, "What Does Image of God Mean," *BioLogos*, accessed April 20, 2025, https://biologos.org/articles/what-does-image-of-god-mean.
2. These gods depicted were Enlil, Shamash, Marduk, Amon-Re, and Horus. For more, I recommend reading Richard Middleton's book, *The Liberating Image: The Imago Dei in Genesis 1* (Grand Rapids, MI: Brazos Press, 2005). It is an amazing academic work that connects the interpretation of the *Imago Dei* in the light of the first chapter of Genesis as well as in relation to ancient Near Eastern cultural context of the image of God and humanity.
3. Richard Middleton, *The Liberating Image: The Imago Dei in Genesis 1* (Grand Rapids, MI: Brazos Press, 2005), 27.

10. DEPOSING THE COUNTERFEIT IDENTITY

1. The Greek word is akathartos (Strong's G169). It is defined the same way by Mounce, Thayer, and Strong's.

A FEW THEOLOGICAL/SCHOLARLY COMMENTS ON MARK 5

1. The third account is found in Matthew 8:28-34.
2. Craig S. Keener, *The IVP Bible Background Commentary: New Testament* (Downers Grove, IL: InterVarsity Press, 1993), 139–140, PDF e-book, https://wnlnetwork.com/wp-content/uploads/2020/10/The-IVP-Bible-Background-Commentary_-New-Testament-2nd-edition-PDFDrive.com-.pdf.
3. Wright, N.T. *Mark for Everyone*. London: Westminster John Knox Press, 2004. https://archive.org/details/markforeveryone0000tomw. Accessed May 1, 2025 through Internet Archive. 55-57.
4. Ibid., 56.

ENDNOTES

11. A SON POWER FLEX

1. Wright, N.T. *Mark for Everyone*. London: Westminster John Knox Press, 2004. https://archive.org/details/markforeveryonen00tomw. Accessed May 1, 2025 through Internet Archive. 55-57.
2. This is counter to many teachings on spiritual warfare, where we are instructed to find the ruling (demonic) spirits in the city, region, nation, and so on. I'm reminded of a statement spoken by my Uncle Cal (Apostle Calvin Cook), of Golden Altar Ministries in San Jose, California. He made the statement that when a sent one of God arrives in a territory, he or she *becomes* the ruling spirit. This scripture certainly bears that out.
3. Jess Thompson, "What Is Quantum Superposition and What Does It Mean for Quantum Computing?," *Live Science*, April 15, 2025, https://www.livescience.com/technology/computing/what-is-quantum-superposition-and-what-does-it-mean-for-quantum-computing.

12. THE STORY OF YOU

1. Donavyn Coffey, "Why Does Christianity Have So Many Denominations?" *Live Science*, last modified July 29, 2022, https://www.livescience.com/christianity-denominations.html.
2. The idea of rewriting your story is one that I attribute to my mom, Dr. Bacer J. Baker. She conducts *Boundless Brain Power* bootcamps, and does an amazing job of helping individuals not only break through mental and emotional barriers, but also come into Kingdom of God manifestations of victory and success. You can find out more about this amazing challenge at www.boundlessbrainpower.com, or you can use my affiliate link: https://boundlessbrainpower.com/join?am_id=

14. SPIRITUAL DISRUPTERS

1. Oxford Languages. S.v. "disrupter." "Accessed December 30, 2024. Google.
2. I am aware of a trend on social media and a number of internet sites, to censor or alter words such as "rape, abuse, sex-trafficked" and the like, using asterisks or dashes in place of certain letters. Possibly one of the reasons is not to traumatize or offend others. This type of censorship is

subject to the publishers of those sites. Truth is ugly in unvarnished states, and personally, I believe that I have shielded the devil's wickedness for too long as it is. If my use of these words offends you, I apologize. No offense is intended; however, I would ask you to please consider that the reality of experiencing the crimes themselves is much uglier than the words on paper. Especially since, even as I type this, there are still too many children (many younger than I was) experiencing this kind of evil on so many more horrendous levels. The true victims need us, the sons of God, to break free of our traumas, so that the real work of rescue and deliverance can manifest for others. And I will pray for you, beloved reader, as well.

3. Bullinger, E. W. *The Companion Bible.* London: Samuel Bagster & Sons, 1922. Appendix 6, "Figures of Speech Used in the Bible." Describes the figure of speech **Metonymy of the Cause**, where Adam's "nakedness" symbolizes the loss of God's glorious likeness, giving new meaning to their knowledge of being naked.

15. THE TRUTH ABOUT BROKENNESS

1. Jeff A. Benner, *Ancient Hebrew Lexicon of the Bible* (College Station, TX: Virtual Bookworm, 2005), s.v. "שלם (shalem)."

   Theological Dictionary of the Old Testament, ed. G. Johannes Botterweck, Helmer Ringgren and Heinz-Josef Fabry, vol. 15 (Grand Rapids, MI: Eerdmans, 1994-1995), s.v. "šālôm," 14–32.

   Francis Brown, S. R. Driver, and Charles A. Briggs, *A Hebrew and English Lexicon of the Old Testament* (Oxford: Clarendon Press, 1906), s.v. "rapha," "tâmîym."

17. BROKEN PIECES & ESTABLISHED PATTERNS

1. I found it interesting that *Nazareth,* according to Thayer's is defined as "the guarded one." In fact, that hit home.

18. REPENTANCE: THE SUPERPOWER OF SONS

1. William D. Mounce, *Mounce's Complete Expository Dictionary of Old*

& *New Testament Words* (Grand Rapids: Zondervan, 2006), s.v. "μετανοέω (*metanoeō*, repent)."

19. A SECOND REPENTANCE SPIRITUAL ENCOUNTER

1. Charles Wesley, "O for a Thousand Tongues to Sing," 1739, public domain. Accessed May 21, 2025. https://hymnary.org/text/o_for_a_thousand_tongues_to_sing.

    The hymn originally had 18 stanzas, and is said to have been written in commemoration of the first anniversary of Charles Wesley's conversion to Christ.

    Robert Lowry, *Nothing But the Blood of Jesus* (1876), hymn originally introduced at a camp meeting in Ocean Grove, New Jersey.
2. Romans 12:1-2 reveals a powerful spirit strategy to help us manifest as obedient sons of the Kingdom of God.

23. THE FREQUENCY OF A GOD-CONTROLLED SPIRIT

1. Bob Dylan, *Gotta Serve Somebody*, track 1 on *Slow Train Coming*, Columbia Records, 1979, vinyl.

APPENDIX A

1. The term quantum faith is a registered term revealed by Annette Capps in her book, *Quantum Faith*®.
2. Annette Capps, *Quantum Faith* (Broken Arrow, OK: Capps Publishing, 2004).

APPENDIX C

1. Jeff A. Benner, *Ancient Hebrew Lexicon of the Bible* (College Station, TX: Virtualbookworm.com Publishing, 2005), Introduction. Paraphrases describing the pictographic origins of Hebrew, its concrete nature, and emphasizes the importance of understanding the ancient Hebrew culture and thought processes when interpreting the biblical text.

About the Author

Lonzine Lee writes for the edification of the Body of Christ and seekers of the Kingdom of God, and works with other authors to do the same thing. She is a pastor, prophetic teacher, writer, worshipper, songwriter, editorial consultant, and aspiring voiceover talent. Pastor Lonzine, also known as PL3 to her Astounding Love family, is passionate about motivating others to seek and live the Kingdom life and to know Christ's love and perfection. She is currently at work on the second book in the K101 Foundations Series, along with accompanying study guides that will help you gain a firm foundation in the teachings and life in the Kingdom of God.

Lonzine honestly believes that the Kingdom of God is the place where you discover and realize the dreams that God has for you. You can trust Him to make His dreams come true. She is a fervent believer that fulfilling your Kingdom destiny manifests healing to the nations. She aims to release *Sonship in Action,* the second book in the Kingdom series in late 2025.

Social media: You can find her on Facebook, LinkedIn, and YouTube. New podcasts and broadcast series coming soon.

- facebook.com/dominionunlimited
- linkedin.com/in/lonzine-lee-mba-5392429
- youtube.com/@DomUnltdMsElle3

BOOKS BY LONZINE L. LEE

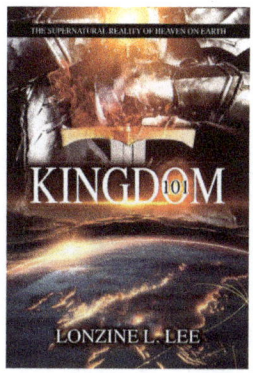

Kingdom 101: The Supernatural Reality of Heaven on Earth

K101 Foundations Series*

Our Quest For Identity - June 2025

Sonship In Action - Winter 2025*

Kingdoms and Kosmos - Spring 2026*

Spirit Words, Frequencies, And Sayings - Summer 2026*

Kingdom Intelligence - Fall 2026*

The Christmas Through The Ages Series

Christmas Through The Ages: Beginning With The First Noel

Christmas Through The Ages: *Do You Hear What I Hear?* - Autumn 2025*

Christmas Through The Ages: *Let Earth Receive Her King!* - Winter 2025*

---

* Anticipated release dates.

THANK YOU!

I hope you enjoyed meeting Reena, the daughter of Herschel and Nessa Hunter, formidable warriors in their own right. These storyline snippets from *Reena's Quest* provide the first peek at the interaction of spirit beings, mortals, mystics, and intrigue in the timeless realm of **Ouranos Ehrets.**

While planning the ***Kingdom 101 (K101) Foundations*** series, the Holy Spirit gave me a nudge to start sharing backstory scenes from my upcoming *Spirit Warrior Trilogy*. At the end of each of the next four books in this series, you'll get a sneak peek into the lives of some of the other characters who are so important to this interactive world. I look forward to sharing more about Ouranos Ehrets with you! See you next time.

Lonzine Lee

www.ingramcontent.com/pod-product-compliance
Lightning Source LLC
Chambersburg PA
CBHW071226170426
43191CB00032B/904